The LAST AMERICANS and

"The Fight for America"

T.C. Brennan

For

The "Last Americans"

TABLE OF CONTENTS

FOREWORD

The Fight for America

Many people might consider the title of this book to be an exaggeration or hyperbolic. You may think so, too. But think back to what we've all just witnessed over the past year during the presidential campaign and especially what we've witnessed since the election and inauguration of our new president.

What we all saw during this time was collusion and corruption on a scale we'd never seen before. Never even imagined before…But… it wasn't between Donald Trump and the Russians (now, almost 9 months after the election of Donald Trump, there is still not ANY evidence of collusion between Trump, or his staff, and the Russian government).

But, there certainly was collusion. And there was corruption. And there was lying and there was cheating and there was a rigged election and there was even a full-fledged conspiracy: to steal the American presidency. *Sounds like a riveting political novel!*

But it wasn't a political novel – it was instead the true story of deceitful, vile, corrupt, arrogant, elitist individuals and entities determined to engineer the outcome of our presidential election to suit their own ends. People, entities and organizations so villainous that one would think they could only come from a political novel. Tragically, they are all too real and they are still very much engaged in these nefarious, anti-American activities: Activities, which are specifically designed to take power away from the people and vest it instead, in the state. And that state, of course, is to be transformed into a socialist/communist "totalitarian" state, in which their party (the Democratic Party) and their president would preside over and rule the country under the aegis of a global world government. This is why they had to try to *steal* the presidency: if told the truth; no one would vote for this.

They (the Democrats) got very close to achieving these goals when they managed to (through fraud and nefarious means) get Barack Obama elected to his presidency.

They were well on their way to their "Nirvana." They almost had it. Obama was doing everything that they wanted him to do: he trampled on the Constitution and was busily dividing and destroying the country in every way he could.

The very fact that they were so close to achieving these goals is precisely why they have all so vehemently and viciously attacked Donald Trump and are willing to do anything to derail him.

Because he intends to undo the gains of their anti-American exploits and give sovereignty back to this country. He ran on this.

This is also why these villains now don't even bother with being fair, or truthful, or to follow the rule of law, or even to be civil. They were too close to their ultimate goal and Trump's election could undo all their gains. Gains that they've been working on for over one hundred years. (See Chapter 5 - What is Progressivism?). They have literally *BECOME CRAZED* over this setback.

To understand this better let's use a common example we can all relate to. Try taking candy away from a child: or ice cream, or their favorite toy... What happens? Now think of the Snowflakes. You get the picture.

So, who are these villains? We all know many of them: At least those that have run for office and those that anchor the news broadcasts and political TV shows. These are obvious, but there are legions more of these subversive, anti-American zealots who have infiltrated and taken over our educational institutions and universities, TV networks, press and media, TV shows, stage shows and movies, the sciences, and un-elected administrative positions in virtually all of our government agencies: and especially, the government's regulatory agencies.

The mass anti-American "indoctrination" by these legions, which has been imposed on our society, is why we are now living in the generation of the *Last Americans*. Those Americans who are already retired or now entering retirement are the last Americans who were honestly educated about this country and know its true role in history.

We now have generations of young adults who have no knowledge of the TRUE HISTORY of The United States or of the huge and noble (yes noble) sacrifices made by this country to free other peoples from the oppression, repression, slavery (yes slavery), genocide and mass murder of the fascist, imperialistic and communist regimes of the twentieth century, which, collectively have been responsible for the torture and deaths of well more than 100 MILLION PEOPLE! *There is no accurate number…*

If you believe the total number of murders attributed to Chinese Communist leader Mao Tse Tung during his purge of the Chinese dissidents during the 1950's and 1960's you can add another 70 million people to this total. North Korea has now murdered more than 20 million of its people.
That we know of…

Instead, these generations (this is the third generation since the late 1960's) have been brainwashed and indoctrinated to believe that the United States has been an evil, selfish, racist country that has exploited the world for its own benefit.

Nothing could be further from the truth.

A Letter To The "American" President

Since you have been elected to be the President of the United States then, we the people, wish make to make an appeal... to you.

We the people of the United States of America appeal to you to truly be: an "American" President.

One, who not only believes in our Constitution, but enforces it, preserves it, and defends it: As your oath of office will call you to do.

One who, like Washington, imposes his virtue on the office, and imbues it with dignity.

One who, like Washington, doesn't forego integrity for the sake of approval, or the doctrines of a party.

One who, like Lincoln, has the courage to do what is right... No Matter What The Cost.

We the people of America appeal to you to be a president who sees us as a whole; and not as classes or races; but as a whole people, for whom our Constitution was written. And we ask you to see each of us individually as the object

of that Constitution: because as individual Americans; each
of is.

We the people, ask you to hold sacred, the trust we place in
you for the governance of our country, and the protection of
it.

And, we the people, ask you to hold America sacred: because
it is.

America can no longer afford political officials who use the
powers entrusted in them to their own ends; or those of a
party; or those of a class; or those of a race; or those of
any other than the whole of us.

America can no longer afford officials in authority, elected
or otherwise, who do their will, and not that of the people.

And...America can no longer afford a president who allows
any of these to happen: even if tacitly.

If you are now elected to be the President of The United
States, you will then need to be... a president of the people,
by the people, and for the people.

You will need to be so because... America needs you to be so.

T. C. Brennan

1-REVISING OUR HISTORY

This is called revisionism or "revisionist history." A term that sounds innocuous and innocent. But it is anything but. The purpose of teaching revisionist history of the United States is to undermine (and eventually) overthrow the United State's (current form of government), and eventually The United States itself, by teaching its youth to hate the country they live in. Indeed, this has worked beyond the wildest dreams of the leftist, progressive, democrats and communists that have forced this "counter-history" into our schools and colleges.

The primary instrument used to replace the country's actual history with the Democratic Left's propaganda was, and is, Education. Education is what could change the hearts and minds of the new generations of Americans. Realizing this, The Democratic Party has made significant efforts to take control of The Department of Education since President Jimmy Carter re-created it and gave it (teeth) federal control over the country's schools and educational curricula. Once the Progressive (LEFTIST) Democrats controlled this federal agency they controlled what the country's students would learn. Before the left took control of this huge agency, education was controlled by the states. The curriculum that was taught then was administered and controlled by the residents of those states. Well, not anymore...

The revisionist history that has been taught in our schools and universities for the last 50 plus years (when history is taught at all) overemphasizes the faults of the United States and erases and eliminates any of the great or positive things that the United States has done throughout its history.

The mistakes of America are portrayed as crimes: the achievements minimized. If mentioned at all.

This is what has been going on for almost sixty years. Is it a wonder then why America's youth hates the country they live in?

After indoctrinating America's students with "Revised anti-American History" the Democrats, Leftist educators and Leftist media use their most successful weapon: "Political Correctness."

This is a tool (created by the Communists), which is used to divide races, classes, genders and income groups and to turn them against each other, and then, to turn them against America. This weapon, in fact, has been the most destructive, debilitating and harmful of all of the weapons that the communists have used against the west and The United States.

We are all victims of allowing our children to be taught, or to be more precise, indoctrinated, by political parties and leftist activists. Political parties are ONLY really interested in seizing power and then keeping that power and its accompanying "Courtiers" life-style of privilege.

This is true of many of the politicians who populate both political parties in The United States. We have all just seen that in spite of the overwhelming elections of Republican candidates at all levels of government, including the Congress in both houses and the presidency that a majority of Republicans are doing nothing to support the new president; Just as they did nothing to stop Barack Obama's flagrantly lawless administration.

And, they have done literally nothing to stop the anti-American propaganda from being taught in our schools and colleges, even though they (the schools) are taxpayer funded institutions and therefore Congress could easily withhold funding from these schools and universities until the practice is discontinued. But, what do they do? Nothing…

This betrayal of the voters IS corruption and those most guilty of this betrayal are the leaders of the party in power, namely Sen. Mitch McConnell and Speaker of the House, Paul Ryan as well as many of the tenured congressmen and women who have been in Washington for far too long.

These "insiders" are content to go along with the Democrats and play both sides of issues as long as the status quo remains in place. John McCain comes to mind...

In addition to the anti-American indoctrination in the schools and colleges, America's youth is also subjected to a constant barrage of anti-American, untrue (propagandist) biased news reporting; which is always critical of anything conservative or patriotic and *never pro-American.*

These last two generations (and especially this most recent) are also the only generations in more than a hundred years that have not been called upon to give up anything for the sake of their country or make any sacrifices for its benefit at all. Instead they have become accustomed to being unaccountable for their actions, not responsible for anything and used to everything that they need being given to them. And, of course, still they want more.

In spite of their privilege, they see themselves as victims: Victims of evil, capitalist America. If, indeed, they do see their privilege (by just being born white for example) they are often willing to publicly self-flagellate to atone for having this evil privilege in the first place.

These lies are reinforced in their minds by a lying, dishonest media and the now totally Leftist Democratic Party, which promises them more free things, and then more free things, for which they do not have to work, or pay for: college for example.

We should all take note that socialist/communist regimes always promised their people that the government would provide free everything to them. It would provide all of their needs. What, of course, they didn't tell those citizens is that communist/socialist governments ALWAYS run out of other people's money and ALWAYS collapse economically: As has Venezuela now and as did the Soviet Union in the 1980's.

And because our college (and now high school) students are only taught the evils of capitalism and never taught the reality of the failures of communism or socialism, they believe the lies and are quick to label capitalism as "evil."

This indoctrination works because they are never, ever taught about the bread lines, or toilet paper shortages, or violence being committed by people who are literally fighting for bare existence in those socialist/communist countries. They are never taught about this.

People in Venezuela are now killing zoo animals for food. Where has that been reported?

And, they are also never taught about the mass murders of dissidents and those who opposed these regimes just as they are never taught about the imprisonment of hundreds of thousands or even millions of people that opposed their socialist/communist governments as well.

Worse yet, they are NEVER taught that the success of capitalism is actually THE REASON they have, not only all of the free things they have, BUT ALL OF THE THINGS that they have (including their smart phones). They're never told that: NEVER, EVER, NEVER….

It is important to remember that most socialist/communist/fascist parties started by "Revising History" as did both The Soviet Union and Nazi Germany. From there they stomped out freedom of speech, freedom of the press, religious freedom and individual liberty: ALL of these are TENETS of the Constitution of The United States. Virtually, all modern totalitarian regimes have started by revising history and then took the subsequent steps noted above. Virtually ALL. We see this today. The radical Islamists (ISIS) are doing it now. They quickly destroy precious antiquities, statues and books everywhere they go. It's one of the first things they do after occupying a territory.

This is important for all of us to remember, but it is much more important that the actual history be put back into the curricula of all of our schools and into the curricula of ALL taxpayer funded colleges and universities and taught to our students in middle schools as well. After all, this IS the REAL history of the world we live in, not what's being taught to our students by Left-leaning teachers and professors for the purposes of political indoctrination and brainwashing.

Americans who love this country should not be complacent about all of this. Revisionist history has worked before in ALL of the regimes that have been mentioned and it is working now. Right here in this country: In the schools in your towns, neighborhoods and the colleges in your cities. These institutions of learning have been taken over and they are the breeding grounds of the Left.

Your children ARE BEING INDOCTRINATED by Left wing anti-American socialist/communist teachers and professors everyday in almost all the colleges in America, in high schools and now even in the lower grades.

Then, political correctness is vigorously "enforced" in the schools, in government and then 24 hours a day in the media and now, even on social media: in short, throughout our entire culture.

By, the way, Political Correctness came from the Communists. It was invented by socialist/communist philosophers in Germany at the Frankfurt School, of Frankfurt, Germany. This was an early Communist think tank/school filled with admirers of Karl Marx.

****

2-TOO YOUNG TO REMEMBER...

Not only are the country's students not taught the true history of America but, almost all of the adults alive in the country today are too young to remember what The United States has done in the world and for the world, particularly, during the twentieth century.

Virtually, all of the adults living in The United States today, and most certainly these last few generations of college students, are too young to remember what really occurred due to the rise of NAZISM in Germany, FASCISM in Italy, IMPERIALISM in Japan and COMMUNISM in Russia and China. They are too young to remember the terrorism, mass imprisonment and mass executions these regimes inflicted upon their own people and then inflicted upon the world as they invaded other countries.

They are too young to remember the millions of American, British, Australian, Canadian, French, Polish, Russian and Chinese lives lost in fighting back, containing, and finally defeating the armies of these horrific regimes in World War II.

Most people are aware of the holocaust (the genocide of the European Jews) in the German concentration camps during World War II throughout Europe. But this subject is treated in our schools almost as a footnote in history, if mentioned at all. There are many teachers and professors now who are teaching students that this never even happened.

Also not taught, is that there were millions of other groups tortured and executed in these camps: Catholics for example: (between 2 to 4 million; no one knows for sure), And there were Poles, Gypsies, Russian prisoners, mentally challenged and handicapped people and hundreds of thousands, and perhaps millions, of political dissidents: Some 14 million in all. And this number is probably low.

Many people think that these numbers are too fantastic to be true. Quite the opposite: consider what Stalin said after he had purged Russia and the Soviet occupied countries of political opponents. "Kill one person, it's a murder. Kill a million… it's a statistic."

And he meant it. *Blood curdling…*

Also essential to realize is that all fascist/socialist/communist states are initially "totalitarian" or quickly become so. They have to. To get people to conform to the repression and deprivations of these forms of government theses regimes have to exert ruthless control over the population.

TOTALITARIAN is a word that many people really don't grasp. In a totalitarian state those that rule the country have all the power. And, it is absolute power. And you? You have nothing. You are not allowed to disagree with the state. If you speak out against the government in any way, you are subject to imprisonment and even execution.

2a-SNOWFLAKES ARE DANGEROUS

The term snowflake refers to this last generation of young adults that are college students and recent grads. These are people who need safe spaces and stuffed animals to cope with society. They, however, are not adults: Young or otherwise. They are really just over-indulged, spoiled *big kids* in adult bodies. Mentally they are at the stage of pre-pubescent children. They are known for their intolerance of anything that upsets them. And, they are easily upset.

So, what upsets them? Everything they disagree with, anything pro-American, anything that requires them to work for what they want and all things Republican, and, or conservative.

So, why are they dangerous, you might ask? Simple: because they can vote. This makes them dangerous. These over-indulged, under achieving brats comprise a huge voting block. It doesn't matter that they are ingrates with no life experience, no work ethic, no wisdom and no appreciation for the sacrifices of others, both past and present, who have enabled them to have the privileges they enjoy. Regardless of all this, these snowflakes still have a huge say in the laws and socio-economic policies of this country.

Unfortunately, with every graduation season that passes America has a new group of millions of these mal-content snowflakes to contend with. Not until Congress gets up the guts or gumption to address the things that are being taught in America's institutions of learning that are outlined in this chapter will the situation improve.

And not until parents stop paying the colleges and universities fantastic sums in tuition, but instead demand that the truth be taught to the their students, instead of the Leftist-Communist indoctrinations, will the colleges stop allowing rogue, Leftist professors to teach their propagandist lies to America's students.

Not good news...

****

3- CONSPIRACIES, LIES AND SEDITION

Sedition is conduct or speech that incites people to rebel against the lawful authority of the state. This is criminal activity. Specifics of the law are delineated in U.S. Code 18-2834.

A conspiracy is a secret plan by a group (of two or more people) to do something harmful or unlawful.

A conspiracy between the Democratic Party and the Mainstream Media against Donald Trump has been underway since the election of 2016. This is not in question. The proof of this conspiracy has already been made public and cannot be disputed. This conspiracy has included false charges against Donald Trump and members of his campaign staff (of collusion with the Russian government to sway the presidential election in Trump's favor) wherein, there has been no evidence shown and no proof offered to substantiate these charges whatsoever over the nine months that these allegations have been under investigation.

The MEDIA, including ABC, CBS, NBC, CNN, The New York Times and The Washington Post have been the main drivers of these false accusations.

Even before the election in November it was known (and proven) that at least 65 prominent broadcast and press journalists from the aforementioned agencies had themselves colluded and conspired with the Clinton Campaign to rig the election in Hillary Clinton's favor!

Since this conspiracy became publicly known those involved in it have not denied their guilt and complicity at all. There is no point in that: It has been proven beyond any doubt. The evidence of their collusion is irrefutable. So here are the people who ACTUALLY

ARE guilty of collusion and conspiracy, accusing Trump and his staff of doing the very things that they themselves were doing!

It, in fact, was Hillary Clinton herself who made up and started this false story (lie) that Trump was colluding with the Russians with absolutely NO EVIDENCE WHATSOEVER to back up these phony claims. Her co-conspirators in the Democratic Party and the media then ran with her lie, relentlessly pushing the narrative and then even embellishing it with additional "made up" false charges: always with information received from "Anonymous Sources."

Before the actual election, during a presidential debate, Hillary Clinton declaratively stated that all 17 intelligence agencies of The United States agreed that there was Russian interference with the election.

This was another lie. *Only four of the U.S. intelligence agencies agreed with her statements and there were only a few "hand-picked" intelligence analysts from only those agencies that went along with Hillary's accusations.*

And it is also very suspicious that it was John Brennan, Obama's CIA Director, who "hand-picked" these analysts. Also noteworthy is that John Brennan has been a member of the Communist Party and reportedly has converted to Islam in recent years.

A constant barrage of charges "leaked" from "anonymous sources" has been the modus operandi of the corrupt media, which are then coupled with more false accusations of members of the Democratic Party at every level.

Never before has America seen a "witch hunt" on this scale with so many conspirators willing and eager to falsely accuse someone and tell outright lies to destroy them in such a blatantly seditious, unlawful and slanderous manner; with absolutely NO facts to back up their charges.

After all of these reporters and conspirators failed to come up with any evidence of the original charge of collusion with the Russians they then created new false charges against Trump, accusing him of obstruction of justice of their investigation of him on the phony charges they made against him in the first place!

This is not just outrageous. It is LUDICROUS. It is SURREAL and it is very much CRIMINAL. Moreover, it is SEDITION and it is a COUP: An unlawful, corrupt coup. We are watching the first serious attempted coup in the history of The United States, being perpetrated by an unscrupulous, and now criminal, political party and its Left-wing co-conspirators (primarily in the media) who are devoid of integrity and any morals or ethics; and none of who have the interests of the voters or the country in mind. At the same time all of these conspirators are inciting violet protests, rioting and civil disobedience all over the country. *This is sedition...*

On the other side of the fence, Donald Trump is receiving no support from his party. Where are his defenders? The Republican leadership is remaining silent while the witch-hunt proceeds. Leading one to wonder why.

Could it be that these Washington Establishment Republican insiders are rooting for the conspirators? Are they in on it? It certainly seems that way to observers of this illegal charade. Will they actually side with the Democrats to illegally impeach Donald Trump, against the will of the people and without cause? Sadly, the answer is: it looks like it.

What we, the voters, are looking at is the usurpation of a duly elected president, our constitution and our form of government.

But, to the evil culprits perpetrating this coup the voters don't matter and the will of the people doesn't matter either.

After all, the type of government they want gives no consideration to the will of the people. Power is the only thing that matters: That, and the fact that *they* have it.

Civil disobedience is the Democrats' newest weapon. This began under Barack Obama in Ferguson Missouri and then again in the city of Baltimore, Maryland, where, in both cases, Barack Obama himself, fomented and encouraged violence and rioting and then justified it, thereby legitimizing it.

Since then Loretta Lynch has called for marches and protests to support resistance against Trump's presidency. And Hillary Clinton's new motto is "resist!" Not, "stop the violence" or anything that would quell the violence. "RESIST!" Which means to resist the new administration. This, of course, just encourages violence from the disgruntled Democratic voters and tacitly endorses the violent ANTIFA mobs of thugs now rampaging all over the country.

The Democrats are quick to call conservatives Nazis but, in fact, it is the Democratic Party that has adopted the fascist tactics of the actual Nazis. And it is the Democratic Party that routinely uses these tactics. Tactics like telling a lie so often that people finally believe it. Tactics like accusing your opponents of doing the very things that you, yourself, are doing: A tactic, which is designed to deflect attention from yourself. These come right out of the Joseph Goebbel's playbook of propaganda and subversion. As do tactics like suppressing free speech and disallowing anyone with differing opinions to speak at all.

And of course, there is the violence being committed by the Leftist mobs running through the streets: which are organized and paid for by the Democratic Party and its operatives.

This is very reminiscent of the violent and brutal "Brown Shirts" of the Nazi Party in Germany during the 1930's.

And, while the vicious charade against Donald Trump continues, the actual malevolent individuals, who have, and are, committing violent, subversive and criminal acts on behalf of The Democratic Party are being exposed one after another; BUT still, face NO CONSEQUENCES. None whatsoever.

All of this and the Republican leadership stands idly by, and… DOES NOTHING! So, are they in on it? *Ask yourself…*

Barack Obama, Hillary Clinton, Loretta Lynch and James Comey have become the un-virtuous paragons of lawlessness, political corruption and civil disobedience.

Obama and Clinton fomented and encouraged violence and rioting and Lynch and Comey broke the law or disregarded it whenever it suited them, usually for political purposes that would help or secure their careers and hurt their political opponents.

Even now, the very people that are investigating Donald Trump are themselves falling under investigation for corruption of their own. Acting FBI Director Andrew McCabe is now under investigation for illegal activities involving his wife's campaign run in Virginia. Apparently, "The Swamp" as it is appropriately called, is even more corrupt than we thought: And a much bigger problem than we thought, too: A lot bigger….

It should be evident to every American now that the government has been entirely and thoroughly corrupted in virtually all of the federal agencies and is being run by a huge, incestuous group of criminals. These people are all in bed with each other, and each is involved in their own scandals. So no one will rat on anyone else. This is why we see no prosecutions, arrests or consequences of any kind for their brazen criminal activities.

This is The Deep State protecting itself. This is also why Donald Trump is such a threat to them and why they have to get rid of him. He not only threatens their lucrative political positions and careers: he threatens their freedom by exposing their criminality. If any honest investigation of all of the individuals involved were to be undertaken by the Trump DOJ these criminal officials, including Loretta Lynch, James Comey and of course, Hillary Clinton herself, would be in prison. So too, would be Barack Obama.

Is it a wonder why there is so much lawlessness? Look at the examples these paragons of authority have set for us. It's simply disgusting… And it is sedition!

****

4-WHAT'S THE ENDGAME?

It's not a mystery. They told us. Democrats have been calling for the impeachment of Donald Trump since *before* his inauguration.

In fact, immediately after the election they started this, calling for his impeachment and his removal from office by ANY MEANS NECESSARY. This is when the Democrats "phony" charges of Russian collusion began. Let us not forget: who these phony collusion charges were started by: Trump's political opponent; Hillary Clinton. *What a surprise...*

Now that the Russian collusion thing has been shown to be bogus, the Democrats are moving on to new accusations and outright lies as fast as they can.

He's innocent of collusion with the Russians? Fine... they'll just make up other charges. They'll find something. Very "Stalinistic." This is what Stalin used to do and that is exactly what is going on right now. And the Democrats (who are being protected by their propagandist media) don't care if their treachery and seditious motives are now obvious. They don't even care if they're caught red-handed in their lies.

This is how brazen they've become. After eight years of Obama and Clinton getting away with their unprecedented treachery and corruption they've learned that they face no consequences for the treasonous behavior that they're engaging in. None whatsoever.

And... Donald Trump? He's like a deer in the headlights. Yes, he's doing what he can to implement his agenda with executive orders and by rescinding many of Obama's unconstitutional and harmful executive orders, but in terms of dealing with these unscrupulous villains and their conspiracy to overthrow him and remove him from office: he's literally doing nothing.

It should have been obvious to him before he even took his oath of office that the first thing he needed to do was to get rid of Obama's implants (appointees and holdovers) from every agency and bureau in D.C.; especially the intelligence services and regulatory agencies.

But, he didn't and he's been paying for that mistake ever since.

He's never going to win them over. Or get them to be fair; or even follow the law. He won't because they hate him. They hate him because he represents a clear and present danger to their agenda. An agenda that calls for open borders, globally controlled world governance instead of America remaining as a sovereign nation with its own constitution and laws and the conversion of America from a free society into a totalitarian, communist state. This is why they hate him…. And us.

Yes, they do hate us. Remember Hillary's statement, "Democratic voters are stupid. They're easy to control." And she said this about her own constituents! Imagine how she thinks of the rest of us. Oh, that's right. She said that too. We're "a basket of deplorables" and we're "irredeemable." These are not just Hillary's opinions, either. Elitist Democrats hold the public in disdain and the media certainly does. People who lie to you do not respect you. The opposite of respect IS disdain.

These people actually think that the fact that they have a college degree from some snarky, elitist school, and a microphone, makes them superior to the rest of us. MSNBC's Rachel Maddow is proof-positive that this is not true.

To be fair, it has to be said that the Republican insiders also hold this view of themselves, and us. Like the Democrats they believe themselves to be elite and they believe us to be just commoners.

Because of this hubris they believe it's OK to lie to us. And they have: repeatedly; Especially since 2009. And they're still doing it right now.

Like myself, there are millions of patriotic Americans who love The United States and believe in its form of government that has done so well by the country for the last 240 years. But what can we do about a government that is being run by unscrupulous, corrupt people in both parties?

George Washington warned about having a political system with only two parties, believing that with only two parties it would be too easy for both to become corrupted.

The answer is that if Donald Trump doesn't do anything about it, then there is simply not much we can do. He was elected to drain the swamp and honestly, he's not doing it. As already stated, he's left the vast makority of the Obama holdovers in their positions. And many of these are decision and policy-making positions.

In addition to this, he (Trump) has appointed a Deputy Attorney General (Rod Rosenstein) who first recommended that he fire James Comey as Director of the FBI and then began investigating him for doing just that: because it "may be" obstruction of justice. May be? What!? The guy's the Deputy Attorney General of The United States and he doesn't know if it's obstruction of justice or not? And if so, why did he recommend firing James Comey in the first place?

Add to this that Trump is allowing himself to be investigated by a "special counsel" (Bob Mueller) who is best friends with James Comey, the man that Trump just fired, and who clearly has an axe to grind with the president. And, Bob Mueller has hired a staff of attorneys to investigate Trump who are Obama and Hillary Clinton supporters and several are even major donors to the Clintons and one, or more, even worked for the Clinton Foundation!

You might be asking yourself what Trump can do about all this and why he's going along with it. Well, actually, there's a lot he can do: If he's willing to buck the establishment Republican insiders along with the media and the Democrats.

But, aside from that, why is Donald Trump allowing himself to be investigated at all? What's is his crime? Make no mistake, the appointment of a special counsel is nothing but a ruse; this so-called "special counsel" IS a special *prosecutor* and is just part of the witch-hunt. Trump is standing by and allowing this to happen, too. More deer in the headlights, I'm sorry to say. But, perhaps he is worried about his own party's support…

As we have all seen, throughout all of these relentless, groundless attacks by the Democrats and their media, the Republican leaders have not exactly been lining up to defend this president. We've seen very little if anything from them. Only a few of the newer or more independent members of the Congress or Senate have defended him at all. And then, it was a tepid defense, to say the least.

Trump is a Republican president, elected by Republican voters and logically speaking, it is a mystery as to why there is no defense of him. There should be a vociferous defense of him by everyone in the GOP, but there isn't. Inexplicable?

Let's not forget that the leaders of the party, the ones with the power and tenure were, for the most part, "Never Trumpers" during the primaries. Some, even after he won the nomination, remained against him. These leaders dictate the party's talking points and what the junior members are allowed to say. Is that what's going on?

Because of this I think it likely that the Republican leadership is waiting to see if a Trump impeachment is going to succeed and, if so, are putting distance between themselves and him, not wanting to be associated with a president tainted by an impeachment. You may not think this to be the case. Unfortunately, I do. I believe that if an impeachment looks as if it could succeed that these RINOS might actually vote for impeachment. *If not that then they will probably just vote "present" and abstain from supporting him.*

However, if Donald Trump should find the guts to buck these establishment insiders who run his party, legally he has complete authority to order that these investigations be stopped, and also the authority to fire anyone in the executive branch for any reason, anytime he wants: including those individuals investigating him.

Of course, if he does this, we all know what the Left-wing media will do and this will bring about immediate cries for impeachment from the all of the Democrats and their low information voters, not to mention the snowflakes; they will be beside themselves!

This will take courage. But, to be a good president does take courage. Now is the time to show it, Mr. Trump.

Additionally, Trump can direct the administrators of the FCC (Federal Communications Commission) to revoke the broadcast licenses of the Networks responsible for this lying, malicious and seditious false reporting. They are engaging in political an actual conspiracy to oust an elected president with a campaign of sedition based on false allegations of (Fake News). And this CAN be proven. TV and radio broadcast networks are legally bound to report THE TRUTH to the public. It is a condition of their broadcasting licenses.

They are NOT allowed to report fake and destructive news stories based on their political positions. The threat of revocation of their broadcasting licenses will put a stop to this treasonous activity. This measure should have been taken a long time ago, but since it wasn't it should be initiated right now in a big way or this won't ever stop.

We have all seen that since Trump did not exercise his authority to thwart these malicious, phony attacks early on, that the media and press just piled on, with more and more unsubstantiated stories from "anonymous sources."

If Trump does nothing he can expect to be harassed by the left and the media incessantly and they will just conjure up new charges to attack him with in their efforts to derail him, if not impeach him, and that threat(impeachment) will always be hanging over his head.

In this event it will be nearly impossible for this president to get his agenda implemented at all, let alone completed.

Because of all of the above and the gravity of the situation it is time for a showdown. In fact, IT"S PAST TIME…

****

5-WHAT IS PROGRESSIVISM?

To borrow a line from the very popular 1982 movie, Poltergeist…
They're… b-a-a-a-c-c-k-k …

Yes they're back. Many people have not noticed how, in 2016, the Democrats started referring to themselves as "progressives" again. Again? Yes, again.

Most people have no idea where this term came from. All of a sudden, in 2016, Hillary Clinton and other prominent Democrats starting calling themselves "Progressives." This term sounds like a modern, slick moniker that the Democrats would typically adopt for themselves: Just as they did with the term Liberal. Which is, when applied to Democrats, exactly the opposite of the truth. There's NOTHING LIBERAL ABOUT LIBERALS.

Actually, politically speaking, it is an old term. Progressivism started in the late 1800s and became very popular in the early part of the 1900s. (Theodore Roosevelt was a Progressive) and fought against the robber barons of the time. He was also instrumental in breaking up the monopolies that the industrial tycoons were busily amassing in the U.S. So, it started off well.

Progressivism was a movement meant to address the abuses and social injustices that came about during the Industrial Revolution of the latter half of the 1800s. Abuses like the severe mistreatment of Irish and Chinese immigrants who built the trans-continental railways in The United States: And, like the nearly universal, cruel and inhumane treatment of the factory workers of the time and of those men that worked in the mines throughout The United States.

Sounds good so far… But…

Americans soon discovered that this movement had been taken over by Communists. Or, perhaps, more correctly: Progressivism had been created by the Communists in the first place, since many of its precepts sounded very much like those espoused by the new Communist Party. It may not have been a coincidence at all that both of these political movements started, became popular and then gained traction at the very same time.

Anyway, it became apparent to those same Americans that the Progressives really had the transformation of the country from a country based on individual liberty to one of socialism, which would eventually lead to Communism, and the suppression of individual liberty, in mind. It became public knowledge that this was the real goal of the Progressives and this, thankfully, was unacceptable with most of the American people of the time.

After all: a huge percent of the population of the U.S. was comprised of immigrants who emigrated to The United States to escape the repression of individual liberty in their own countries, which were, for the most part, still monarchies with kings, queens, dukes and duchesses. Most European countries were still not much more than quasi-democracies in the late 1800s.

And…it was to escape these countries, and for individual rights and liberties, that the immigrants had come here in the first place.

Several Progressive candidates ran for office in the first half of the twentieth century, but found that they could not get themselves elected to virtually any office. Soon thereafter the movement lost its popularity and by 1924 it was all but gone from the political scene in the country. And, Democrats of all stripes immediately distanced themselves from anything called Progressive. The name itself had become a stigma. This remained the case for many years, until the election season of 2016, that is.

So, then why did the Democrats start openly calling themselves Progressives again in 2016? They did because they saw themselves as having largely succeeded in transforming The United States of America into a socialist/communistic state due to the flagrantly unconstitutional, forced transitional initiatives, regulations and policies of Barrack Hussein Obama and his administration.

The Democrats incorrectly thought that the American people liked Barack Obama's anti-American socialistic policies and that they had fully embraced this forced socialism. In this they were very wrong. The plain truth is that Americans decidedly didn't like his policies, were resentful of his regulations, and frankly, distinctly resented and disliked him as well.

When polled as to Obama's popularity, Americans would lie to protect themselves, and the pollsters and media, always lied to show Obama in a positive light. People were afraid to speak the truth about Barrack Obama, or to criticize him in any way, because they were afraid that they would be accused of being racist, which of course they would. This was a tactic of the media throughout Obama's terms of office. It still is.

We would all do well to remember that ALL the polls showed Hillary Clinton as winning the presidential election by a wide margin. It was supposed to be a landslide.. After all, Hillary was running on the policies of the ever so popular, Barack Obama. Plus… the election was rigged!

There simply is no good reason to trust the pollsters anymore.

Democrats don't yet realize how much they have been burned by the lawlessness of Barack Obama and Hillary Clinton. It's hard to find anyone who has anything good to say about Obama now, even amongst those that voted for him. People who supported Hillary can't find anything good to say about her, either. (The truth is out).

They either voted for Hillary simply because she was a woman, or simply because she was the Democratic candidate. Even now, no one, it seems, is able to articulate any valid reason for voting for Hillary.

Elections are a much better way to measure the public's view of a candidate than any polls. 2010, 2012, 2014 & 2016: all sweeps for Republicans at all levels of government and disasters for the Democrats.

So much for the Democrats "coming out" as the Progressives they are. But, then again, Democrats don't let go easily.

And the Democrats still don't realize that this last presidential election was a repudiation of Barack Obama and his policies. Hillary ran on a platform of continuing those policies and then expanding them. And now we have learned that indeed there was widespread voter fraud and that Hillary may not have actually won the popular vote, either. It is now suspected that there were literally millions of fraudulent votes cast for Hillary Clinton by the Democratic Party operatives nationwide. *What a surprise...*

Also surprising and even, astounding, is that the leaders of the Democratic Party are still calling themselves "Progressives." And pushing it's corresponding agenda of correcting social injustices.

Correcting Social Injustices: uh-oh – We all know what that means. It means denying your heritage, your culture, your religion and political beliefs. It means giving up things like your freedom of speech, your right to assembly, your privacy, your right to face those that accuse you of crimes, your second amendment right to own arms and, of course, your right to keep the money you earn or property you acquire.

It means giving up all of this: Unless, of course, you're a Muslim, or black, or Hispanic, or gay, or lesbian, or transgender, or bi, or an illegal immigrant, or a refugee, or a single parent (but then only if you're a female single parent). If you're any of these, then you get to keep all of these things and then you get to impose your views, your beliefs, your way of life and your will on everyone else in society. And if anyone offends you… you get to have the U.S. government sue them and destroy their lives, plus you get a nice, undeserved financial settlement, too.

This is modern "Progressivism" and this is the REAL Democratic Party: Today's Democratic Party.

If you think these examples are an exaggeration: think again.

During the Obama Administration the owners of bakeries and restaurants were sued, their businesses and lives destroyed by federal lawyers and judges for refusing (on religious grounds) to cater for or participate in arrangements for gay weddings and other events that were contrary to their religious beliefs.

Catholic nuns who were engaged in charitable work were sued for not providing condoms to the employees of their organization.

It's an ironic fact that the very first settlers who came to this country to start new lives, and a new country, came here because of the religious persecution they faced in the countries they left.

****

6-THE DEEP STATE

What Is The Deep State?

A little bit of history is in order here...

The United States Constitution delineates 3 distinct branches of government: The Executive branch, the Legislative branch (this includes both houses of Congress) and the Judiciary, which is our court system; headed by the Supreme Court.

But, for some time now, there has existed a 4th branch of the government, which has, in fact, become the largest branch of our government and is responsible for most of the laws, regulations and policies that affect our everyday lives, yet it is not mentioned in The Constitution of The United States at all. On top of that: none of the people who run this 4th branch of the government have been elected to their positions; in fact, they have never run for an elected office at all. They have been appointed.

The creation of a fourth branch of government was never envisaged or mentioned by the creators of our Constitution. So, you might be asking yourselves just how this fourth branch of government came into being.

This, most execrable of all, 4th branch of our federal government has been created by our politicians over the years, (usually presidents, and or, congressmen). This branch is referred to today as the "Administrative Branch," though it is not formally called that.

As a matter of fact, it is not recognized as a distinct branch of the government at all. But, this is the branch of our government where all of the regulatory Departments and Agencies are: Like the IRS, the EPA, the FBI, the DEA the Departments of Commerce,

Education, Transportation, Energy, etc. *It would take several pages to list them all.*

Within this 4th branch of government and these agencies are more than 2.8 million federal government employees, none of which have been elected to their positions, either. This is just short of having one federal government employee for every citizen in the country.

I assure you, none of the founders of this country ever imagined a monstrous bureaucracy of this size. Quite to the contrary: They constantly warned against it. The Constitution itself was designed to limit the size and the power of the federal government. Our government has now become the antithesis of that design.

This huge bureaucracy is home to the operatives of the, so-called, Deep State. Within the regulatory departments and agencies of this odious administrative branch are legions of pencil-wielding, mini-monarchs who believe, that since they work for the government, they have the right and authority to tell you and I what to do and how to live. The regulations and policies that these people write become the De facto laws of The United States. It is the onerous regulations imposed by these people that President Trump has been rescinding through his executive orders.

Of course it is not every staff level employee who is to blame. But each of these agencies and departments has Directors, Deputy-Directors, Assistant Deputy-Directors and so on. This is where the Deep State operates. These "middle-managers" are the people who actually create, write and enforce the policies and regulations that we all have to live with. And, far too many of these people are appointed to their positions by the Party in power. Unfortunately, most of them have agendas. Agendas, that are, decidedly not conducive to a free United States of America.

These are the people that Donald Trump has not taken the time to get rid of and consequently they are still enforcing the onerous policies of Barack Obama.

We have all recently seen some of these agenda-driven operatives of the Deep State abusing the power of their office to persecute, and then even to penalize, people and organizations of opposing political persuasions. Lois Lerner (a perfect example of a Deep Sate operative) and the IRS's illegal and deliberate targeting and persecution of legitimate conservative organizations during the Obama Administration comes to mind. This is but one example. Sadly, there are many others.

****

7-THE COMING INSURRECTION: Civil War 2.0

Yes, insurrection: And, yes, Civil War. This is Plan B for the Leftists and The Democratic Party if they cannot get Trump impeached and then, get a Left-wing Democrat back in the Whitehouse. They want control of our government: The whole government. This must, of course, include the presidency.

Too, far out, you think…? Can't happen here… Never happen in America… Well, it's already happening and it has been happening since the presidential campaign back in 2016. And even before that. Actually, it has been happening since Barack Obama was elected to his second term.

The Democratic Party has been actively engaging in acts of civil disobedience and yes, insurrection, for some time. But, this was ratcheted up throughout the summer and fall of 2016, while the presidential campaigns were underway. The Democrats and anti-American communists and socialists (such as George Soros) had been paying for agitators and rioters to infiltrate Trump campaign rallies and violently disrupt them with acts of violence, mayhem and destruction directed towards the legitimate attendees of those rallies. They have also recently paid for agitators to violently disrupt Republican Town Hall meetings held by GOP congressmen and women. And the Democratic operatives have also paid for agitators and rioters to violently protest and riot at colleges and universities or any venues where conservatives are scheduled to speak. We all saw this happen in Berkeley when Charles Murray was scheduled to speak there recently.

Before ANTIFA (the current paid insurrectionist group) there was Black Lives Matter; before that there was Occupy Wall Street. All, have been, or currently are, funded by the Democrats and their affiliates and co-conspirators.

How do we know this? Because the ads that the Leftists ran to hire the agitators (which included their pay rates) have been published on the Internet and have also been exposed on national TV. And the hires' handbooks containing the instructions on how to disrupt these events and cause mayhem have been made public as well. The handbooks further instructed the paid agitators to say that they were Republicans and/or Trump supporters (during those rallies).

And, the Left-wing media does their part to support this violent insurrection. They omit reporting on the ads for rioters paid for by the Democrats (a lie of omission is still a lie) and falsely report that the violence is because of Trump's hate-speech: or his policies.

It would not surprise me at all if it were found that the CIA (under the direction of Barack Obama and John Brennan) was behind some, or much, of this agitation, rioting and violent insurrection: Especially if it would help to advance Obama's pathological mania about racism in America.

Clearly, Obama endorsed the violence at Ferguson, Missouri in 2015. He actually incited it by legitimizing the reason for it. He never made any statements disavowing the false claims of "hands up, don't shoot" even after his own Justice Department (headed by a black Attorney General) spent weeks investigating the incident and found that it was the black youth who had instigated the whole thing and that the "hands up, don't shoot" rendition of what happened between police officer Darren Wilson and thug Michael Brown was nothing but a lie. A lie drummed up to fan the flames of racism (Obama's pet cause).

It is also well known that violent agitators were bussed in to riot in Ferguson. The same is true for Baltimore's insurrection. So, no, it wouldn't surprise me.

Add to all this that Obama met personally with the chief organizer of the paid agitators many times in the Whitehouse. So many times that it was obvious that Barack Obama himself was personally involved in organizing these terrorist events. He also invited the organizers of Black Lives Matter to the Whitehouse and heaped praise upon these racist thugs for spewing their lies and hatred. Obama was an agitator, as well as being a community organizer, so it would not be at all surprising that he would be involved in these activities or with these groups.

Up to now, conservatives and Republicans have been, for the most part, and with rare exception, if not silent, very quiet about all of this Democratic Party corruption and mayhem. This is amazing considering that they have put up with eight years of the constant lawlessness, corruption, lies and destructive and unconstitutional actions of the Democratic Party's fraudulent president, Barrack Obama.

But now, the Democrats are pushing the envelope. These aren't demonstrations. We're used to demonstrations in America. These are violent acts of deliberate insurrection. And if the Democrats continue to push for insurrection, and keep exacting violence against law abiding citizens, and if these Democrats keep rioting and causing mayhem, and if this president is driven from office for fallacious and partisan, political reasons; there will be a reckoning. And it won't be just at the voting both.

The shooting war and violence has, so far, been one sided. The violence has come exclusively from the Left. The Democratic Party has fomented and encouraged this just as Hillary Clinton is doing now: RESIST! Never do the Democrats speak out against these violent, rioting protesters. Never do they condemn these criminals. Instead, they and the corrupt media try to switch the blame to the conservatives and Republicans for inciting the violence and the lawlessness. But, it is not the conservatives, nor the Republicans that are taking out ads to hire agitators and rioters to cause mayhem and destruction all over the country.

To stop this lawlessness our government has to get to the root of the problem. They have to bring the organizers of this mayhem to justice and prosecute them for organizing and inciting riots and for seditious activities. These insurrectionists must be prosecuted and jailed and the politicians involved should be jailed as well. That is the only way to put a stop to this violent, destructive behavior, short of a violent conservative backlash.

No one should be surprised by anything that the Democrats and Leftists do now. There is nothing they won't do to wrest power back from the conservatives that have now taken office. Nothing. They will literally do anything to get their power back, lawless or not. With Barack Obama they had total and unbridled power in their grasp and this reversal of fortune has made them desperate to get that power back. They are not going to accept a conservatively run government during Trump's term in office: or even if he should get another term. They have made it quite clear that, rather than have a conservative in the Whitehouse, they would have a CIVIL WAR.

For those who think the previous paragraph to be hyperbole or histrionics: think again. Once before the Democratic Party went "berserk" over the election of a Republican president: Only once. And who was that president? It was Abraham Lincoln. It was his very election that prompted the secession of the Southern states (they were all Democratic back then) and the commencement of the Civil War. And why was that? Lincoln was against slavery...

Today, black racists and Leftist academics are revising this actual history to say that this is not true of Lincoln and that slavery wasn't the reason for the Civil War. WRONG.

8- GETTING RID OF GOD – The Godlessness of The Left

Some readers may object to such strong terms. They might find calling the Left godless as an exaggeration, or even to be just hysterical rhetoric.

Well… it is neither. Not in the least. The Democratic Party is responsible for removing God from our culture and our society everywhere they could over the last 40 to 50 years. They have been responsible for removing God, or the mention of God, from our public buildings, from documents, from public spaces and worst of all: from our schools. The mention of God has systematically been removed from textbooks and the History Department Curriculums in most of America's schools.

One of the tenets of virtually all of the totalitarian governments that have existed in the world over the past century is that there can be NO tolerance of a belief in GOD. God must be removed from the hearts and minds of the people.

This was done autocratically, by force, in the Soviet Union in the early part of the twentieth century.

The reason for this is simple: God and God's laws represent a higher moral authority than man and most certainly higher than the political leaders or laws of a country. In a fascist, totalitarian state, the state can be the ONLY authority. Hence: NO GOD.

In The United States getting rid of God is being accomplished in two ways. First through revisionist history that teaches wrongly and incorrectly about the so-called separation of church and state clause in America's constitution and second, through the courts and organizations like the ACLU (American Civil Liberties Union) and all types of left wing activists and, of course, the contemporary Democratic Party itself, which mendaciously promotes the "false" argument that the Constitution specifies that there be a "separation of church and state," which it does not. Nowhere in the founding document does it specify the separation of church and state.

What it does state, with respect to religion, is this: "Congress shall make no law respecting an establishment of religion, or prohibiting the free exercise thereof."

The meaning of the two statements contained in this clause of the First Amendment of The United States Constitution (commonly referred to as The Establishment Clause) have been deliberately twisted and perverted by the Left and the Democratic Party to mean the opposite of what they actually do mean.

"Congress shall make no law respecting an establishment of religion" in the vernacular of the day, meant that the government shall not endorse a religion or require a belief in any religion. It meant nothing more than that. It did not mean that the government was to prohibit religion from anything to do with the governance of the country or the proceedings of government.

It is a fact that both houses of our congress (both the Senate and The House) started every one of their sessions with both prayer and readings from *what they themselves called* The Holy Bible. And, of course, these were the very same men that wrote the Constitution of The United States in the first place.

"Prohibiting the free exercise thereof" means simply that our government cannot prohibit or interfere with the practice of any religion or belief in it.

These definitions are quite different than what has been taught in our schools and colleges by Leftist teachers and educators for the past 60 years. What has been taught, and what is taught now, is just more revisionist history about The United States. Which, obviously is anything but the truth.

But, this perversion of the "Establishment Clause" is always the starting point for the Democratic Party's campaign to "Get Rid of God" from our society and even from our culture. (The Left and the Democratic Party have become synonymous now: they have been since the Obama presidency.)

Efforts of the modern Democratic Party and other Leftists to get rid of God and religion are, for now, directed at Judaism and Christianity. The moral imperatives and principles advocated by Judaism and Christianity just don't wash with the morals of the modern Democratic Party. On the contrary, they interfere with them

For Example:

You can't be "humanist" and believe in God, or even gods. To be a humanist is to believe that humans have complete sovereignty over themselves. There is no need for a god. Any god. As humans we're smart enough and good enough to control our own destinies and to decide what is right and wrong: moral and immoral for our society. God is not needed, or even wanted, for that matter. We, not God, are in control and we're doing just fine, thank you very much...

Humanism is yet another new "philosophy du jour" of the liberal academics and the political left.

It might seem to you that I'm talking about atheists. And, in part, I am. Atheists are definitely welcome in the modern Democratic Party and many atheists naturally gravitate to the Democratic Party for obvious reasons. Also, a lot of the atheists initiate lawsuits on their own to stamp out God from public spaces, government buildings, cemeteries (yes, even cemeteries) and the like, which of course is very much welcomed by the socialistic/communist Left.

The effort to get God out of society has become all the more urgent because of The Democratic Party's stance on modern day issues like abortion, LBGT lifestyles and other issues having to do with lifestyle choices, which do not comport with the teachings in the Bible.

On June 18, 1963 the U.S. Supreme Court ruled that the reading of the Bible and the recital of prayer in schools was unconstitutional and therefore, illegal. This was the beginning of America's War against God, which manifested itself then, and continues now, as a war on Christianity due to that religion's preeminence in America. It also commenced the efforts of the Left to eliminate God, or the mention of God, from all spheres of our culture and society. This court decision was a huge victory for atheists and of course for, the political Left.

To the Leftists this Supreme Court decision was validation of their belief that God has no place in our society AT ALL. Since then they have waged a war using the lower courts to penalize people who have religious convictions and try to adhere to them in their everyday lives or especially, in the course of conducting their businesses.

But, the inconsistencies of the Democrats, especially when it comes to religion and feminism (another liberal cause du jour) are glaring. They consider the tenets of Judaism and Christianity to be harsh, if not Draconian, and definitely outdated.

Archaic would be a good word to use here.

But at the same time they are not only tolerant of, but, welcoming to, Muslim immigrants from the mid-east whose customs and religious beliefs call for the subjugation of women, for genital mutilation of women, for honor killings (the murder of a usually female child by a father or mother for dishonoring the family) and for the brutal executions of gays, lesbians, bisexuals and even the children of non-believers (like Christians) by crucifixions and the burning of people alive and, or beheading them. (Yes, I said children; even very young children).

And yet, the Democrats don't criticize Muslims for these hideous and barbarous behaviors. So, why is that? They say it's because of "moral relativism." Moral relativism? Oh my God, yet another "lofty" term from the academics of the Democratic Left.

But, what does it mean? It means that whether a belief, or an act, is right or wrong: moral or immoral; is really determined by the culture from which it comes and that we should not impose our values upon those beliefs or the acts resulting from them: The subjugation of women for example, or marriage to little girls. These are ignored because of moral relativism. The logic is that it's a Muslim thing, or a black thing, or a Hispanic thing. Depends on the group. Anyway, you get the picture…

But, the real answer is simple. The enemy in the way of the Democratic Left for the past century that has been the biggest impediment to the advancement of their ultra liberal, secular, socialist society, (and that they have been desperately trying to get rid of) is Christianity (and Judaism to a lesser degree).

Fundamentalist Islam is completely at odds with these religions and their teachings. Therefore: "The enemy of my enemy, is my friend." This is why these Islamic practices aren't criticized.

So there's that, and the fact that Christianity is the religion upon which The United States was founded. This… is really the heart of the matter.

Integral to the socialist/communist utopia (actually dystopia) that the Democrats want is that God is NOT PART OF IT.

If one examines the many movements within the Democratic Party today it becomes self-evident that many of these issues are actually driven by resentment towards God and the belief in Him.

Make no mistake: it is a secular society that they want, and only a secular society.

Recent court cases over the last eight years have shown that many of the factions of the Left have been encouraged to file lawsuits, which attack various tenets and customs of the Judeo-Christian faiths, particularly those having to do with homosexuality and marriage.

****

9-WHAT SHOULD DONALD TRUMP BE DOING NOW?

Many Trump supporters are outraged by the abuses heaped on
Donald Trump every single day and all night; every single night.
They are fiercely indignant that a president is being treated this
way by broadcasters in the news business, who, have maliciously
lied about him in an effort to remove him from office. The Trump
supporters are infuriated and want something done. *Where are the
Republicans?*

But, equally infuriated, and MUCH MORE frustrated, are the
Leftists, Liberals and Democrats who have been launching these
unfounded and fallacious assaults against President Trump 24
hours a day.

This is almost funny to watch because they accuse Trump of being
an egotistical jerk and narcissist without even realizing it is the ego
and narcissism of Donald Trump that makes him so impervious to
their attacks. It doesn't matter what they throw at him or say about
him; nothing works. It all just bounces off him as if he's the Iron-
man. Ironically, it is the huge ego of Donald Trump that is his
armor. Also ironic, is that it is doubtful that any of the other 16
Republican candidates who ran for president could, or would, have
stood up to these relentless assaults by the Left wing press and
media. Most of them, with the exception of Ted Cruz, have been
quick to tuck tail when attacked by the media at all, much less the
way Trump has been.

 Regardless of this, Donald Trump should, of course, be continuing
with his agenda. This is what he promised the American people
and this is what the country desperately needs. But, Trump does
need to deal with the Obama implants and holdovers and other
"Deep Staters" who are deliberately trying to keep the President's
agenda from being put into effect or even implemented at all, and

who infest all agencies of the federal government now; including both houses of Congress.

Our government is actually running on auto pilot now, with the Obama holdovers still in charge: running the agencie; that actually run our government.

President Trump and his cabinet need to do a "housecleaning" much more aggressively than they have to date. If they don't many of Trump's "key" campaign promises will never come to fruition: The wall for example. Donald Trump even has GOP opposition to this measure and this opposition is, unfortunately, centered in the Republican leadership. Namely: Speaker of the House, Paul Ryan. Ryan, as well as Mitch McConnell, and any of the other rogue Republicans have to be brought into line with the Trump's agenda. *John McCain comes to mind. Again...*

And of course, there are foreign policy initiatives and "critical" national security issues to deal with. Not that you'd know it based on the mainstream media's headlines or the Democratic Party's talking points. They are still only interested in attacking Donald Trump. And they're doing it at the expense of our national security!

Donald Trump should be free to laser-focus on critical national threats like North Korea. But instead his cabinet has to deal with the constant attacks and lies of the Leftist Democratic Party and their complicit media. This shows us all their TRUE priorities.

They are not interested in the security of the United States at all, or the security of its people for that matter. Those things are NOT their priorities. The Democrats and liberals are SO OBSESSED with getting their power back and removing Trump from office that they have lost any sense of reason and would literally put this country, and the American people, in jeopardy to accomplish their seditious and treasonous ambitions. This, in fact, is exactly what they are doing.

President Trump must address this situation quickly. He has let it linger too long and the situation will not remedy itself. He has to get rid of "the snakes in the tent" now and bring this rogue Leftist media into line.

It was NOT Donald Trump who came up with the campaign slogan of "Drain the Swamp." It was the supporters who showed up at his rallies that came up with that battle cry. Once he saw how popular it was, he adopted it. Nevertheless, his supporters now expect him to drain the swamp to bring some order and lawfulness back to the government of this country.

Sadly, Donald Trump is not expending near enough energy to clean up this problem. The "swamp" is not only alive and well: it is thriving! And these swamp creatures will continue to impede the implementation of Trump's agenda and plague his presidency until he addresses the problem fully.

****

10-WHAT SHOULD CONGRESS BE DOING?

Something would be good. Anything to support this president would be better yet. But, the Republican Congress, or at least the congressional leadership of the Republicans, has done little to support this president or his agenda.

Neither have they bothered to defend this Republican president (who, by the way, won in a landslide) from the atrocious attacks of the Left and the corrupt, dishonest media. These anti-American Leftists have had free reign to insult, harass and harangue Donald Trump and all the while the Republicans in office have not lifted a finger to help him.

Since the GOP congress hasn't had the gumption to do either of the aforementioned things they, at the very least, should stop screwing around with the existing health care bill and stop trying to appease Obama's supporters by trying to fix it. Rather, they should repeal it right now: immediately. Every word of it!

It is a disgrace, both to Republicans and to the country, that after being given the majorities in both the House and then the Senate, the Republicans elected to these offices did not have a replacement bill ready to replace Obama's abomination that was passed by the Democrats in 2010. They had EIGHT YEARS! It was 8 long years during which they repeatedly bragged and crowed about having written numerous bills to repeal Barack Obama's Affordable Care Act. Well, where are they?

Of course, they don't exist. Clearly there was NO INTENTION of repealing Obama Care at all. And consequently, no replacement bill was ever written. One can only conclude from this that the Republican leadership and the Congressmen and women that have been in D.C. for any length of time, were just giving the voters more lip service. Along with that obvious conclusion we should also conclude that MANY in the Republican establishment are "Deep Staters," more interested in protecting that Deep State and the status quo than doing the will of the people, which they had promised they would do. Oh, that's right: that was before the election…

With this kind of resistance and betrayal you might well be asking yourself: what can we do? Or, what should we do now?

There is currently a lot of buzz on social media about having a Convention of States, which is described in ARTICLE V of the Constitution. This article of The Constitution was designed to give the states and the voters a way to limit the size and scope of the federal government and reign in its power if need be.

But the practicality of it succeeding is doubtful. The Constitution and ARTICLE V stipulate that new amendments or changes to existing amendments need to have approval of two-thirds majorities in both houses of Congress.

Currently, Congress can't even get a simple one-vote majority for the simplest of things. The likelihood of a two-thirds majority in both houses seems beyond reach, especially if it were for measures that would strip them of their own power.

Even before that: for a Convention of States to be convened at all requires that the legislatures of two thirds of the states vote to hold the convention. Needless to say, this will be a long and arduous process; if indeed, it is possible at all.

All of us should keep in mind that many of the Washington elitists and Deep Staters (Statists) are not doing the will of the people because they have different agenda in mind that they are allegiant to.

Their allegiance is to the One World Government Globalists and it is that socialist agenda (based on the European model) that they are working to fulfill.

Therefore, the problem has to be left up to the states.

****

11-WHAT SHOULD WE DO NOW?

Due to the malfeasance of our government officials and since
voting for Republicans has proven to be futile, we, the people,
have but one remedy left. We must take the power back from this
government, which is so rife with corruption, Deep Staters and
partisanship.

As already mentioned, the Constitutional method of doing this is
called a Convention of States and is described in ARTICLE V of
The United States Constitution. But due to the difficulties involved
in convening a Convention of the States we have to find other
ways to get the job done.

TERM LIMITS for those who hold public office at the federal
level is a good start and there are also calls for this now. But, keep
in mind that this measure requires that the very people who would
be subject to term limits vote for them.

Nonetheless, unceasing pressure should be put on Congress and the
Senate right now to enact term limits or the problem will never be
solved. Our best bet though, is to only elect candidates who do
promise to vote for term limits and not to elect any candidate who
does not.

RECALL INITIATIVES are another good way of holding elected
officials accountable to the voters. BUT, Constitutionally, there is
no way to do this: Senators and, or, Congresspersons cannot be
recalled, even by the people who voted for them.

This is a serious shortcoming of our constitution but to change it
means that we're back to getting a constitutional amendment
passed by the very people it would negatively affect. This is
enough of a reason to hold a Convention of States by itself.

Unfortunately, for all of us, our best shot is still at the voting booth. These efforts should start with NOT re-electing any of the elitist Washington insiders. Like Paul Ryan, Mitch McConnell or John McCain (there he is again) to name just a few.

****

12-WHAT'S REALLY GOING ON HERE?

What's really going on here is a fight to the death for America
itself and just who will control it: Leftist Communist Democrats or
Americans who love their country, believe in its constitution and
want to keep it.

Having Barack Obama in office for eight years is the closest the
Leftist Democrats and Progressives have come to taking over The
United States in 150 years of trying. What we are seeing are the
Democrats and Progressives desperately using every weapon and
tactic they have to wrest control of this country back to themselves.

You might be asking yourself why they are acting so viciously. It's
because they and their Party are in their death throes. They have
been found out: AGAIN.

As they see it, they almost had it all. If they let Trump's agenda go
through now the country will turn around and the agenda that they
forced on us for eight years will be exposed as nothing but a heap
of lies. Lies designed to force Americans to accept what they
called, "The New Normal." Anyone remember that?

All during Obama's imperious reign, every time there was more
bad news, (which was daily) he and his media sycophants would
get on TV and chime in that this is the "new normal" and that we
have to accept it.

In this fight the Leftists, Progressives and Democrats (all the same
now) don't care at all if what they are doing is legal or illegal, right
or wrong, fair or unfair, civil or uncivil. This is war to them: A war
for the control and transformation of America into their socialist,
communist, totalitarian state, which is to be just one part of a vast
world government controlled by elitists in Europe.

This indeed, is what the European Union was, and is, about. And, it's what BREXIT was about. The Brexit movement was about British citizens saying NO to a world government run by un-elected officials in another country deciding what laws would be imposed in Britain.

It was about British citizens saying NO to the forced immigration of thousands of Muslim migrants into their country.

America and "Americanism" are the biggest barriers to a world government, run by Europeans. This is why there is so much support from Europe and Europeans for the Left and the Democratic Party.

Today, unknown and un-elected individuals in Brussels are running the countries in Europe: And the citizens of those countries.

The people of the individual countries in Europe have little, if anything, to say about the laws and regulations imposed on them by the European Union officials in Brussels. All the laws and regulations are passed by fiat. The people have no recourse, but to live with them.

Europeans, in essence, have become serfs again. This is what's really going on here. This is what the Leftists and Democrats really want. The Europeans are already, largely serfs: the Americans are to be next. That's why Hillary Clinton was running around the country saying that she was going to completely eliminate the borders of The United States! Completely! She proudly touted this during her campaign. We are to be world citizens: not American citizens.

Of course, the Leftists, Progressives and Democrats will deny this and even ridicule the assertions made in this book. Of course they will. You can count on it. What do criminals and charlatans always do when confronted with their lies, crimes and misdeeds? They *always* vociferously deny them and immediately go on the attack. They aggressively, maliciously and fallaciously attack and ridicule their accusers. They slander and demean them in every way they can and they use every dirty tactic they can to besmirch their accusers thereby diverting attention from themselves until the heat blows over. How many times have we seen that this past year? How many times have the Democrats done these very things?

These Leftist Democrats and Progressives have done so much damage to our country that much of it is now irreparable and cannot be reversed. We have already lost the last three generations of Americans that were noted in the first chapter of this book. It will take years to get them back; if we are able to at all.

And while we are figuring out what to do another generation is at risk. Every time our students enter our high schools they are really entering indoctrination camps for the Left and will be subjected to anti-American propaganda on a daily basis. The colleges are even worse.

In fact, our children are well on their way to being indoctrinated before they ever step foot in our high schools. Even young children are now challenging their parents about left wing propaganda that they learn in grammar school and on social media.

But we should all remember that things in this country were also quite bad in 1979 when Jimmy Carter was president, at least until the 1980 election. Ronald Reagan reversed this. He made America, America again.

So, the question is: Can Donald Trump do what Ronald Reagan did? Is he divined to be the one that sets America straight again?

We'll all have to wait and see, but right now one thing's for sure. He's in the fight of his life and we are in the fight of our lives.

****

13-IS AMERICA GOD'S COUNTRY? WAS IT EVER?

Many people today (usually Americans) are fond of saying that America is 'God's Country." They believe that God had a hand in the founding and creation of The United States of America and that He has guided it and protected it since its inception.

Could that be true? Could God have actually played a role in the creation of this country? Has He protected it throughout its history? Was God responsible for producing the phenomenal leaders that have led this country through its times of peril and turmoil?

Provable or not, this country seems to have benefited from some kind of divine intervention (what Washington called "providence") since even before it was founded in 1776.

Long before America was settled and well more than a century before The United States declared itself to be an independent nation things occurred here that defy explanation: Things that simply could not have happened, but for some kind of "Divine Intervention."

 On the pages that follow are highly improbable yet absolutely true stories about this country and some of the people who prominently played vital roles in its history.

These stories have been selected from my upcoming factual book and video "America, God's Country: Is It Really? Was It Ever?"

I've chosen these accounts to show that there were, indeed, people who did experience some form of "Divine Intervention" and that America itself benefited from these interventions as well.

****

George Washington

The Indispensable Man

Many historians and biographers have called George Washington "the" indispensable man, without whom, the American Revolution and War for Independence from England would not likely have succeeded.

Furthermore, they state, that the country itself might have failed in its first years without George Washington's leadership.

Most Americans know very little about this very fascinating man. He truly was unique and he truly did benefit from some kind of favor from above or "providence" as he called it.

The following story will give you a taste of what I'm referring to. For the sake of brevity, I've kept the story short and covered just the salient points.

****

There was a war in America before America was The United States and before our Revolutionary War. This war is known as The French and Indian War, which occurred twenty years before our revolution in 1776.

Don't worry; I won't get mired in the history here except to say:

Both the French and British had many settlements in America at that time and both countries were engaged in a fight for control of the American colonies and territories.

It was in a battle during this war that one George Washington rose from obscurity and got his "street cred" as a military officer.

Here's the story:

This battle occurred in 1755 near the Monongahela River in Pennsylvania. George Washington was, at the time, an officer of the Virginia Militia, which supplemented the British army in its engagements in the region. It was this army that was attacked by the French and their Indian allies on July 9th of that year.

During this battle ALL of the officers of the British army were either killed or wounded, including General Edward Braddock, the commanding general of the British. ALL the officers that is, except for one: George Washington. This was quite surprising: especially to the Indians. They had specifically targeted him, in particular, as he was such a tall and imposing figure sitting atop his horse in the middle of the British troops.

The Indians had been firing at near point blank distances from Washington and still he did not fall. These Indian warriors became quite perplexed by this. They were all experienced hunters and warriors. But they could not hit him. Even the Indian chief had himself fired at Washington in an effort to fell him from his horse. Eleven times he tried: at close range. Still Washington did not fall, even though two horses had been shot out from under him during the fierce fighting.

This battle was a massacre. The British lost 1,000 of their 1,400 men that day.

Finally, as the Indians continued to try and hit Washington, the chief raised his hand and ordered his warriors to stop firing at him. Many of the Indians were angry with their chief over this order. Washington was in their sights, right in front of them, and they were determined to kill this one last officer of the enemy.

After the battle Washington noted in a letter to a friend that his hat had two holes shot in it and his that coat had numerous holes, but not one shot ever penetrated his body. He had survived the battle unscathed.

Washington credited this to providence (the protection of the Divine).

****

Many years later, when George Washington was president, he was touring cities in the Northeastern states. On this trip, now President Washington came upon an elderly Indian who desperately wanted to speak with him. It was in fact, the Chief of the Indian warriors who had fought against the British Army at Monongahela in 1755.

This Indian chief had walked some three hundred miles through extremely severe winter storms to meet the new president, so important was the message he had for George Washington.

During their conversation the Indian Chief told Washington an astounding story.

The Chief explained to Washington that during the battle, both he and his warriors were determined to kill him, but after repeated unsuccessful attempts the Chief received a mysterious message from above.

According to the Indian, the Great Father had communicated
directly with him... about Washington.

I've paraphrased the message below.

"Do no harm to this man. For he is to be
The Father of a great nation, yet unborn."

****

The preceding account is true and it is just one of numerous
providential things that happened to people who were involved in
the foundation and creation of The United States of America.

As a matter of fact, this story about George Washington is but one
of many that actually did happen to him and there were several
more incidents where the father of the country should have been
killed in battle, but, through some miracle... wasn't.

Washington continually displayed unrivalled bravery (to the point
of being reckless) in battle many times, yet he never got a scratch
throughout the 8 years and numerous battles of the Revolutionary
War.

Was Washington's good fortune just chance, or sheer luck? Well...
not according to the Indian Chief.

****

After the war George Washington was (virtually) unanimously elected to be the first president of The United States. Four years later he was again nearly unanimously re-elected.

Four years after that the people of America wanted Washington to be the ruling monarch of America and assume the title and position of KING of The United States. But Washington magnanimously declined this honor. He then also declined the election to a third term as the president. Washington believed that an individual in power too long posed risks to the new republican democracy that was The United States of America.

****

The Pilgrims

We've all learned about the Pilgrims in grammar school; or we thought we did. But the most astonishing aspect of their experience was left out of our schoolbooks and from the story our teachers told us in grade school.

When the Pilgrims landed in Massachusetts, at the place they later named Plymouth, they met a solitary Indian man, who befriended them and then helped them through their first winter in the New World. This is pretty much what we all learned. It's a great story.

But... here's the REAL story:

That one Indian, called Squanto, (his actual name was actually Tisquantum) did meet and befriend the Pilgrims. He was not only friendly towards them, but didn't seem to fear them at all, as did most Native Americans when meeting Europeans. But why was that?

Here's the part that was left out of our schoolbooks...

The Pilgrims were indeed happy to be befriended by this Native-American man. But they were even happier when they found out that this particular Indian spoke very good English to boot!

What luck... The Pilgrims were English.

Well, not exactly… It wasn't luck.

It turns out that Squanto had been educated and taught to speak English by Europeans while living in Europe for several years.

What!? *I know what you're thinking…*

How in the world could an American Indian have lived in Europe, of all places?

The Indian explained to the Pilgrims that he had been abducted by Spanish explorers many years before and brought back to Europe to be sold as a slave.

Upon learning of this, Spanish monks raised the money to buy the Indian's freedom and took him into their monastery, where they cared for and educated him. Later they even raised the money for Squanto to book passage to get back to his native land and his native people.

However, when Squanto finally did return to America he found that his tribe had disappeared. He concluded that they had either moved to find another territory or had died from disease. Their fate was unknown to him and he had no idea where they were or if they were alive.

So, he stayed where he was. And this enabled him to meet up with the Pilgrims: This, and the fact that the Pilgrim's ship (called the Mayflower) had landed at Plymouth only by accident. In fact, it was only by accident that they landed in Massachusetts at all. They had planned to land much further south down the Atlantic coast.

According to the ship's records, the Mayflower encountered severe stormy weather as they approached the Americas and they were blown off course. The captain of the Mayflower decided to land where he did because of the location's bay and good landing portage and beaches.

He wanted no part of any further exploration on the coast and insisted that the Pilgrims de-board where they could. It turned out that it was at Plymouth; right where Squanto was.

So that's the true story of the Pilgrims and their Indian helper, Squanto.

Not exactly a chance meeting. This took some doing…

Divine Intervention…?

Think of all the things that had to happen, when they happened, for this Indian to meet the Pilgrims. And, think of the odds that this one Indian, this particular Indian, would speak the language of the Pilgrims: That and the fact that if the Mayflower hadn't run into storms and been blown off course, the Pilgrims would have never met this Indian at all.

****

By the way… the first form of government the Pilgrims established when they settled in Plymouth, Massachusetts was communism: before it was known as communism. The Pilgrim leaders set up a "commune" where everyone would share equally in the resources of the new colony.

It failed miserably within months. The Pilgrims soon learned that some people were willing to work and some weren't. Many of their party just "leeched" off the productive members of the colony.

This caused great resentment between those who worked and produced things and those who didn't. So, the Pilgrims abandoned "communism" for good.

Abraham Lincoln's
Mysterious Birth
and
who was Sarah Parsons?

In 1809 Kentucky was at the western edge of The United States. This was still considered the frontier at the time. Nevertheless, many Americans moved to this territory to set up homesteads and start a new life of their own there, as did Thomas and Nancy Lincoln. They had a small farm on a patch of land about 45 miles from Lexington. It was pretty much in the middle of nowhere at the time and it wasn't much. Just a small cabin on an otherwise non-descript, flat piece of dirt for as far as the eye could see. *This will be important as the story progresses.*

On February 11th of that year, Nancy was due to give birth to her second child. However, all that day she was having difficulty and severe pain. She and her husband Thomas suspected that the baby was not positioned right in the womb for birth and they became increasingly concerned. A breech delivery was virtually a death sentence for both mother and baby at that time. They needed help.

After several hours Thomas raced into the small town closest to them to get the aid of a doctor or midwife for the delivery. But, he was unsuccessful in getting any help at all. The midwife had left the day before to aid another woman with her delivery and the town's doctor could not be found. Thomas returned home quite dispirited.

As the day stretched into evening Thomas grew more and more frantic as Nancy's labor got even more difficult than it had been. By now the couple was almost sure that this would be a breech birth and that even if, by the grace of God, the baby did survive, Nancy probably would not. The situation was grim.

It was about this time that a mysterious woman appeared at their front door. She introduced herself as Sarah Parsons and said that she was a midwife and that she had come to help, whereupon she immediately began to tend to Nancy.

It was a long, arduous and painful labor for Nancy Lincoln. The two women worked for hours on end without relief. Finally, very late that night a baby boy was born and thankfully, he appeared to be healthy and normal. Nancy also had survived the birth and looked to be fine. The midwife sat with them the rest of that long night looking after mother and baby.

In the morning the midwife assured Thomas that his wife and new baby boy would be fine and then announced that she had to leave. Thomas urged her to wait so that he could give her money in payment for her life-saving services, but when he offered her the money the enigmatic woman said that she had no need of money and that she just needed to go. Thomas persisted and asked what he could do for her: He was insistent that he do something in return for her services.

She looked at him directly and, after a pause, asked him to promise her that he would name his son Abraham. Thomas was surprised at the request, but quickly agreed. With that she turned and walked out the door. Both Nancy and Thomas were quite surprised by the abrupt departure of this mysterious woman.

Nancy insisted that Thomas to go after the woman and give her money for her services whether she wanted it or not. But, seconds later, when Thomas walked outside the cabin, the woman had disappeared. He looked in both directions down the long road that ran past their home. All the land surrounding the cabin in every direction was extremely flat. There is no way this woman could have disappeared so quickly, he thought to himself.

****

Word had gotten around town that Thomas Lincoln's wife needed help to deliver her baby and hours later that day the town doctor came to the Lincoln's door. He was delighted to see that mother and baby were fine.

He asked how they had managed the delivery, since he had heard that Nancy Lincoln was having difficulty. He was astounded when the Lincoln's told him about the mysterious appearance of the midwife the night before. He was even more astounded when he learned that the woman was Sarah Parsons.

"Sarah Parsons, why that's impossible!" he declared. Then he divulged to the Lincolns that Sarah Parsons had been tragically killed on her way to deliver another baby the very day before. He, himself, had been called out of town to the accident scene and examined Sarah Parsons personally. She was most certainly dead and therefore could not possibly have shown up to deliver the Lincoln's baby.

The doctor was perplexed but left convinced that the Lincolns had been mistaken. He knew that Sarah Parsons was dead.

****

The story about the Lincolns and the mysterious appearance of
Sarah Parsons, the midwife, is, of course, anecdotal. The only two
witnesses to Sarah Parsons having been there at all were Thomas
and Nancy Lincoln.

However, the story about Washington at Monongahela and the
story of the Pilgrims and Tisquantum have been verified with the
official records of the British Army, the fastidious records of
George Washington himself and the detailed records that were
recorded by the Pilgrims.

****

14-WHAT ABOUT DIVINE INTERVENTION?

You might be skeptical about these stories of God's intervention. After all they happened a long time ago. The story of the Pilgrims was 400 years ago, Washington's story was 260 years ago and the story about Lincoln was over two hundred years ago. You might be thinking, "What has God done for us lately?

Well, here's a story of "Divine Intervention" that happened much more recently. I can vouch for the veracity of this story: because it happened to me and there is not a word of exaggeration in the account you are about to read. It involves a thirteen year old girl, a Yankee baseball hat, me and, of course, God. These events occurred almost thirty years ago when I was living in Chicago.

At the time I had a business in which I was a paid consultant for the owners of retail apparel stores. My job was to teach the owners how to make their stores more profitable and to avoid losing any money. As a consequence of my job I worked in, and was familiar with, most of the retail malls in the Chicago metropolitan area. *This will become important as the story progresses.*

The thirteen-year old girl was my daughter, Chelsey, who was living in New York with her mom. Because of the long distance between us her visits were rare and it had been a while since I had seen her last, so I was anxiously looking forward to this visit to spend some time with her. But, there was still a month to go before she arrived so I tried my best to contain my excitement until the day she came.

Around this time, for whatever reason, I got it in my head that I wanted to get a Yankee baseball hat. I had been a die-hard Yankee fan as a little boy and for some reason I just had to have a Yankee baseball hat now.

Everyday as I made my rounds to my client's stores in the malls I made sure to check every sporting goods and department store in each mall to see if they had one in stock. Sure enough there were plenty of Yankee hats. But they were not authentic Yankee hats and this just would not do. Not for me at least. I was determined to get myself an authentic Yankee hat. Like the kind I wanted when I was a kid, but never got.

The Yankee hats these stores had were every kind of blue but Yankee blue. (Yankee blue is a dark, dark, almost black, indigo blue.) These hats were every kind of blue BUT indigo blue. They were turquoise blue, navy blue, even powder blue. Powder blue…? But, they were not the Yankee blue. Anyway, I kept checking the stores everyday for most of that month. And everyday I got the same result. No Yankee hat.

I didn't pray for this, but I did talk to God about it daily. Every day: The entire day. You might think I was borderline obsessed about getting this authentic Yankee hat. But then again, at that time in my life I talked to God about everything. Everything: all day long: everyday.

As the days passed by with the same result, I gradually starting letting go of my desire for this Yankee hat and began to come to grips with not finding one: At least not one that was authentic. I had several conversations with God about it and let him know that I was OK with not getting my Yankee hat.

I was also very much conscious of the fact, that God probably thought that I should be thinking more about my daughter's visit and less about the hat. But, then again, I knew that He knew very well that I was thinking about my daughter anyhow.

Finally the big day came. My daughter's plane was coming in early and it was landing at O'Hare so I knew that place would be very crowded. (It always is) so I got there early. I hoped her plane would not be late: I couldn't wait to see my kid. Finally the plane arrived and the passengers de-boarded into the gate area.

Even though I was a long way away form the gate area I could see my daughter. Teenaged girls in the late 1980's wore some pretty outlandish hairstyles (Watch a 1980's movie and you'll see.) And my daughter's hairstyle was outlandish and then some so, she was easily spotted by me as she walked out of the gate area and started towards me down the long passageway to the terminal.

She was still quite far away but I could see that she was carrying a large duffle bag instead of typical luggage. As she got closer I could see that there was something attached to the outside of the duffle bag. But she was still too far away for me to make out what it was. I could only see that it was dark. Very dark: almost black.

Finally she reached me and we gave each other a H-U-G-E hug. When we were done hugging each other and I looked down I could see that the object pinned to the outside of her duffle bag was a dark, indigo blue Yankee hat. I did a double take.

She saw me looking at it with a stunned expression on my face and quickly explained (not sure whether I would like it or not) that she brought it along to give to me, but that if I didn't like it she would just throw it away. *Are you kidding, I thought to myself.*

I asked her what made her think of bringing me a baseball hat.

Here's the story behind it…

It turns out that my daughter Chelsey's best friend was being taken for a day out… by her dad… to a baseball game and she had to go. This girl desperately pleaded with my daughter to go through the insufferable ordeal with her and go along. (After all they were best

friends.) So, Chelsey went along with her friend and her friend's
dad to… Yankee Stadium. It also turned out that it happened to be
"Hat Day" where the Yankees give out free hats to all the fans in
attendance for the game that day.

So there it was. While I was running around through malls trying
to find an authentic Yankee hat my daughter had gone to Yankee
Stadium with her friend and gotten a free "authentic-real'"" Yankee
baseball cap from the New York Yankees themselves, at Yankee
Stadium!

After all the details of how many things had to happen (all of
which were beyond my control and beyond my daughter's
knowledge) for this hat to get to me sank in I just looked up and
shook my head. I should have known, I thought to myself.

I spent a lot of time thanking God for this one… Thanking him and
thinking of just how awesome He is…

I've only told this story to a very few people. I simply call it, "The
Yankee Hat Story." Clearly, it was not a simple story at all. It
required a lot of Divine Intervention. These things simply could
not have happened by themselves.

****

There are those that believe in the power of intention. That our
intentions can actually make things happen. Bring our wishes to
fruition. (Jesus did) and I do, too) But, in this case, it was never my
intention to have my daughter or anyone else get me a Yankee hat.
This was something that I had talked to God about. And only God.

****

Postscript

There are many more stories of "Divine Intervention" that have occurred throughout America's history and that were essential to its creation. Those accounts will be elaborated on in "America: God's Country" when it comes out later this year.

At this point, though, I'd like to take the time to make you aware of the fact that before this recent presidential election there were predictions made by people who profess to have received prophetic messages from above: messages concerning Donald Trump. The prophecies were that he would win the presidential election and become the next president of The United States. There were three such predictions (or prophecies) that were notable that I know of.

Two of these prophecies came from men who are people of deep religious conviction, but not known as prophets.

However, one of these men was a very well known prophet. His name was Kim Clement. Mr. Clement has passed on recently, but long before the 2016 presidential election he had made predictions concerning Trump. He was the very first person I know of to make predictions about Donald Trump and the American presidency. These messages (prophecies) were made almost a decade before Donald Trump was even on the radar screen in terms of running for the presidency.

It was all the way back in 2007 that Kim Clement first received a prophetic message about Trump while on stage in front of several thousands of people at a concert. He was being videotaped when he received, what he said, was a prophetic message from above. "Trump shall become a trumpet" was one of the notable phrases from that prophecy. *This video is online.*

Since 2007 Kim Clements received many more prophetic messages about the new president to be: Donald Trump, although Trump was not often mentioned by his full name in those prophecies.

The videos of these subsequent prophecies are also online. One in particular, from April 4th 2014 will give you chills as will the first video from 2007. Most surprising is that each of the subsequent prophecies and videos that followed the original in 2007 seem to get more and more specific, even talking about the Left's calls for impeachment and things we are now seeing with the media. Also mentioned, were the Democratic Party's scandals that occurred in the run up to the election, last fall.

To any of you reading this I strongly recommend watching Kim Clement's prophetic videos about Trump and about Hillary, which were made in 2016, long before the election, though.

Indeed, Kim Clement received many prophetic messages about Trump and this recent presidential election, however, they came about because Kim Clement had been praying about the future of America… and Israel.

Finally, Republican politicians would do well to watch these videos and take heed: the author of these messages does not speak well of them, either.

****

BIBLIOGRAPHY and UN-NAMED SOURCES

In keeping with the new precedent set by the major publishers of news in The United States (The Washington Post, Time Magazine, The New York Times, etc.) the author has elected to use only the information obtained from "anonymous" or "unnamed" sources for the writing of this book. The following pages list those sources.

****

The Constitution of
The United States of America
(Passed by Congress in 1787)

We the People of the United States, in Order to form a more perfect Union, establish Justice, insure domestic Tranquility, provide for the common defence, promote the general Welfare, and secure the Blessings of Liberty to ourselves and our Posterity, do ordain and establish this Constitution for the United States of America.

Article 1.

Section 1

All legislative Powers herein granted shall be vested in a Congress of the United States, which shall consist of a Senate and House of Representatives.

Section 2

The House of Representatives shall be composed of Members chosen every second Year by the People of the several States, and the Electors in each State shall have the Qualifications requisite for Electors of the most numerous Branch of the State Legislature.

No Person shall be a Representative who shall not have attained to the Age of twenty five Years, and been seven Years a Citizen of the United States, and who shall not, when elected, be an Inhabitant of that State in which he shall be chosen.

Representatives and direct Taxes shall be apportioned among the several States which may be included within this Union, according to their respective Numbers, which shall be determined by adding to the whole Number of free Persons, including those bound to Service for a Term of Years, and excluding Indians not taxed, three fifths of all other Persons.

The actual Enumeration shall be made within three Years after the first Meeting of the Congress of the United States, and within every subsequent Term of ten Years, in such Manner as they shall by Law direct. The Number of Representatives shall not exceed one for every thirty Thousand, but each State shall have at Least one Representative; and until such enumeration shall be made, the State of New Hampshire shall be entitled to choose three, Massachusetts eight, Rhode Island and Providence Plantations one, Connecticut five, New York six, New Jersey four, Pennsylvania eight, Delaware one, Maryland six, Virginia ten, North Carolina five, South Carolina five and Georgia three.When vacancies happen in the Representation from any State, the Executive Authority thereof shall issue Writs of Election to fill such Vacancies.

The House of Representatives shall choose their Speaker and other Officers; and shall have the sole Power of Impeachment.

Section 3

The Senate of the United States shall be composed of two Senators from each State, chosen by the Legislature thereof, for six Years; and each Senator shall have one Vote.

Immediately after they shall be assembled in Consequence of the first Election, they shall be divided as equally as may be into three Classes. The Seats of the Senators of the first Class shall be vacated at the Expiration of the second Year, of the second Class at the Expiration of the fourth Year, and of the third Class at the Expiration of the sixth Year, so that one third may be chosen every second Year; and if Vacancies happen by Resignation, or otherwise, during the Recess of the Legislature of any State, the Executive thereof may make temporary Appointments until the next Meeting of the Legislature, which shall then fill such Vacancies.

No person shall be a Senator who shall not have attained to the Age of thirty Years, and been nine Years a Citizen of the United States, and who shall not, when elected, be an Inhabitant of that State for which he shall be chosen.

The Vice President of the United States shall be President of the Senate, but shall have no Vote, unless they be equally divided.

The Senate shall choose their other Officers, and also a President pro tempore, in the absence of the Vice President, or when he shall exercise the Office of President of the United States.

The Senate shall have the sole Power to try all Impeachments. When sitting for that Purpose, they shall be on Oath or Affirmation. When the President of the United States is tried, the Chief Justice shall preside: And no Person shall be convicted without the Concurrence of two thirds of the Members present.

Judgment in Cases of Impeachment shall not extend further than to removal from Office, and disqualification to hold and enjoy any Office of honor, Trust or Profit under the United States: but the Party convicted shall nevertheless be liable and subject to Indictment, Trial, Judgment and Punishment, according to Law.

Section 4

The Times, Places and Manner of holding Elections for Senators and Representatives, shall be prescribed in each State by the Legislature thereof; but the Congress may at any time by Law make or alter such Regulations, except as to the Place of Choosing Senators.

The Congress shall assemble at least once in every Year, and such Meeting shall be on the first Monday in December, unless they shall by Law appoint a
different Day.

Section 5

Each House shall be the Judge of the Elections, Returns and Qualifications of its own Members, and a Majority of each shall constitute a Quorum to do Business; but a smaller number may adjourn from day to day, and may be authorized to compel the Attendance of absent Members, in such Manner, and under such Penalties as each House may provide.

Each House may determine the Rules of its Proceedings, punish its Members for disorderly Behavior, and, with the Concurrence of two-thirds, expel a Member.

Each House shall keep a Journal of its Proceedings, and from time to time publish the same, excepting such Parts as may in their Judgment require Secrecy; and the Yeas and Nays of the Members of either House on any question shall, at the Desire of one fifth of those Present, be entered on the Journal.

Neither House, during the Session of Congress, shall, without the Consent of the other, adjourn for more than three days, nor to any other Place than that in which the two Houses shall be sitting.

Section 6

The Senators and Representatives shall receive a Compensation for their Services, to be ascertained by Law, and paid out of the Treasury of the United States. They shall in all Cases, except Treason, Felony and Breach of the Peace, be privileged from Arrest during their Attendance at the Session of their respective Houses, and in going to and returning from the same; and for any Speech or Debate in either House, they shall not be questioned in any other Place.

No Senator or Representative shall, during the Time for which he was elected, be appointed to any civil Office under the Authority of the United States which shall have been created, or the Emoluments whereof shall have been increased during such time; and no Person holding any Office under the United States, shall be a Member of either House during his Continuance in Office.

Section 7

All bills for raising Revenue shall originate in the House of Representatives; but the Senate may propose or concur with Amendments as on other Bills.

Every Bill which shall have passed the House of Representatives and the Senate, shall, before it become a Law, be presented to the President of the United States; If he approve he shall sign it, but if not he shall return it, with his Objections to that House in which it shall have originated, who shall enter the Objections at large on their Journal, and proceed to reconsider it. If after such Reconsideration two thirds of that House shall agree to pass the Bill, it shall be sent, together with the Objections, to the other

House, by which it shall likewise be reconsidered, and if approved by two thirds of that House, it shall become a Law. But in all such Cases the Votes of both Houses shall be determined byYeas and Nays, and the Names of the Persons voting for and against the Bill shall be entered on the Journal of each House respectively. If any Bill shall not be returned by the President within ten Days (Sundays excepted) after it shall have been presented to him, the Same shall be a Law, in like Manner as if he had signed it, unless the Congress by their Adjournment prevent its Return, in which Case it shall not be a Law.

Every Order, Resolution, or Vote to which the Concurrence of the Senate and House of Representatives may be necessary (except on a question of Adjournment) shall be presented to the President of the United States; and before the Same shall take Effect, shall be approved by him, or being disapproved by him, shall be repassed by two thirds of the Senate and House of Representatives, according to the Rules and Limitations prescribed in the Case of a Bill.

Section 8

The Congress shall have Power To lay and collect Taxes, Duties, Imposts and Excises, to pay the Debts and provide for the common Defence and generalWelfare of the United States; but all Duties, Imposts and Excises shall be uniform throughout the United States; To borrow money on the credit of the United States;

To regulate Commerce with foreign Nations, and among the several States, and with the Indian Tribes; To establish an uniform Rule of Naturalization, and uniform Laws on the subject of Bankruptcies throughout the United States;

To coin Money, regulate the Value thereof, and of foreign Coin, and fix the Standard of Weights and Measures;

To provide for the Punishment of counterfeiting the Securities and current Coin of the United States;

To establish Post Offices and Post Roads;

To promote the Progress of Science and useful Arts, by securing for limited Times to Authors and Inventors the exclusive Right to their respective Writings and Discoveries;

To constitute Tribunals inferior to the supreme Court;

To define and punish Piracies and Felonies committed on the high Seas, and Offenses against the Law of Nations;

To declare War, grant Letters of Marque and Reprisal, and make Rules concerning Captures on Land and Water;

To raise and support Armies, but no Appropriation of Money to that Use shall be for a longer Term than two Years;

To provide and maintain a Navy;

To make Rules for the Government and Regulation of the land and naval Forces;

To provide for calling forth the Militia to execute the Laws of the Union, suppress Insurrections and repel Invasions;

To provide for organizing, arming, and disciplining, the Militia, and for governing such Part of them as may be employed in the Service of the United States, reserving to the States respectively, the Appointment of the Officers, and the Authority of training the Militia according to the discipline prescribed by Congress;

To exercise exclusive Legislation in all Cases whatsoever, over such District (not exceeding ten Miles square) as may, by Cession of particular States, and the acceptance of Congress, become the Seat of the Government of the United States, and to exercise like Authority over all Places purchased by the Consent of the Legislature of the State in which the Same shall be, for the Erection of Forts, Magazines, Arsenals, dock-Yards, and other needful Buildings; And To make all Laws which shall be necessary and proper for carrying into Execution the foregoing Powers, and all other Powers vested by this Constitution in the Government of the United States, or in any Department or Officer thereof.

Section 9

The Migration or Importation of such Persons as any of the States now existing shall think proper to admit, shall not be prohibited by the Congress prior to the Year one thousand eight hundred and eight, but a tax or duty may be imposed on such Importation, not exceeding ten dollars for each Person.

The privilege of the Writ of Habeas Corpus shall not be suspended, unless when in Cases of Rebellion or Invasion the public Safety may require it.

No Bill of Attainder or ex post facto Law shall be passed.

No capitation, or other direct, Tax shall be laid, unless in Proportion to the Census or Enumeration herein before directed to be taken.

No Tax or Duty shall be laid on Articles exported from any State.

No Preference shall be given by any Regulation of Commerce or Revenue to the Ports of one State over those of another: nor shall Vessels bound to, or from, one State, be obliged to enter, clear, or pay Duties in another.

No Money shall be drawn from the Treasury, but in Consequence of Appropriations made by Law; and a regular Statement and Account of the Receipts and
Expenditures of all public Money shall be published from time to time.

No Title of Nobility shall be granted by the United States: And no Person holding any Office of Profit or Trust under them, shall, without the Consent of the Congress, accept of any present, Emolument, Office, or Title, of any kind whatever, from any King, Prince or foreign State.

Section 10

No State shall enter into any Treaty, Alliance, or Confederation; grant Letters of Marque and Reprisal; coin Money; emit Bills of Credit; make any Thing but
gold and silver Coin a Tender in Payment of Debts; pass any Bill of Attainder, ex post facto Law, or Law impairing the Obligation of Contracts, or grant any
Title of Nobility.

No State shall, without the Consent of the Congress, lay any Imposts or Duties on Imports or Exports, except what may be absolutely necessary for executing its inspection Laws: and the net Produce of all Duties and Imposts, laid by any State on Imports or Exports, shall be for the Use of the Treasury of the United States;

and all such Laws shall be subject to the Revision and Control of the Congress.

No State shall, without the Consent of Congress, lay any duty of Tonnage, keep Troops, or Ships of War in time of Peace, enter into any Agreement or Compact with another State, or with a foreign Power, or engage in War, unless actually invaded, or in such imminent Danger as will not admit of delay.

Article 2.

Section 1

The executive Power shall be vested in a President of the United States of America. He shall hold his Office during the Term of four Years, and, together with the Vice-President chosen for the same Term, be elected, as follows:

Each State shall appoint, in such Manner as the Legislature thereof may direct, a Number of Electors, equal to the whole Number of Senators and Representatives to which the State may be entitled in the Congress: but no Senator or Representative, or Person holding an Office of Trust or Profit under the United States, shall be appointed an Elector.

The Electors shall meet in their respective States, and vote by Ballot for two persons, of whom one at least shall not lie an Inhabitant of the same State with themselves. And they shall make a List of all the Persons voted for, and of the Number of Votes for each; which List they shall sign and certify, and transmit sealed to the Seat of the Government of the United States, directed to the President of the Senate. The President of the Senate shall, in the Presence of the Senate and House of Representatives, open all the

Certificates, and the Votes shall then be counted. The Person having the greatest Number of Votes shall be the President, if such Number be a Majority of the whole Number of Electors appointed; and if there be more than one who have such Majority, and have an equal Number of Votes, then the House of Representatives shall immediately choose by Ballot one of them for President; and if no Person have aMajority, then from the five highest on the List the said House shall in like Manner choose the President. But in choosing the President, the Votes shall be taken by States, the Representation from each State having one Vote; a quorum for this Purpose shall consist of a Member or Members from two-thirds of the States, and a Majority of all the States shall be necessary to a Choice. In every Case, after the Choice of the President, the Person having the greatest Number of Votes of the Electors shall be the Vice President. But if there should remain two or more who have equal Votes, the Senate shall choose from them by Ballot the Vice-President.

The Congress may determine the Time of choosing the Electors, and the Day on which they shall give their Votes; which Day shall be the same throughout the United States.

No person except a natural born Citizen, or a Citizen of the United States, at the time of the Adoption of this Constitution, shall be eligible to the Office of President; neither shall any Person be eligible to that Office who shall not have attained to the Age of thirty-five Years, and been fourteen Years a Resident within the United States.

In Case of the Removal of the President from Office, or of his Death, Resignation, or Inability to discharge the Powers and Duties of the said Office, the same shall devolve on the Vice President, and the Congress may by Law provide for the Case of Removal, Death, Resignation or Inability, both of the President and Vice President, declaring what Officer shall then act as President, and such Officer shall act accordingly, until the Disability be removed, or a President shall be elected.

The President shall, at stated Times, receive for his Services, a Compensation, which shall neither be increased nor diminished during the Period for which he shall have been elected, and he shall not receive within that Period any other Emolument from the United States, or any of them.

Before he enter on the Execution of his Office, he shall take the following Oath or Affirmation:

"I do solemnly swear (or affirm) that I will faithfully execute the Office of President of the United States, and will to the best of my Ability, preserve, protect and defend the Constitution of the United States."

Section 2

The President shall be Commander in Chief of the Army and Navy of the United States, and of the Militia of the several States, when called into the actual
Service of the United States; he may require the Opinion, in writing, of the principal Officer in each of the executive Departments, upon any subject relating to the Duties of their respective Offices, and he shall have Power to Grant Reprieves and Pardons for Offenses against the United States, except in Cases of Impeachment.

He shall have Power, by and with the Advice and Consent of the Senate, to make Treaties, provided two thirds of the Senators present concur; and he shall nominate, and by and with the Advice and Consent of the Senate, shall appoint Ambassadors, other public Ministers and Consuls, Judges of the supreme Court, and all other Officers of the United States, whose Appointments are not herein otherwise provided for, and which shall be established by Law: but the Congress may by Law vest the Appointment of such inferior Officers, as they think proper, in the President alone, in the Courts of Law, or in the Heads of Departments.

The President shall have Power to fill up all Vacancies that may happen during the Recess of the Senate, by granting Commissions, which shall expire at the End of their next Session.

Section 3

He shall from time to time give to the Congress Information of the State of the Union, and recommend to their Consideration such Measures as he shall judge necessary and expedient; he may, on extraordinary Occasions, convene both Houses, or either of them, and in Case of Disagreement between them, with Respect to the Time of Adjournment, he may adjourn them to such Time as he shall think proper; he shall receive Ambassadors and other public Ministers; he shall take Care that the Laws be faithfully executed, and shall Commission all the Officers of the United States.

Section 4

The President, Vice President and all civil Officers of the United States, shall be removed from Office on Impeachment for, and Conviction of, Treason, Bribery, or other high Crimes and Misdemeanors.

Article 3.

Section 1

The judicial Power of the United States, shall be vested in one supreme Court, and in such inferior Courts as the Congress may from time to time ordain and establish. The Judges, both of the supreme and inferior Courts, shall hold their Offices during good Behavior, and shall, at stated Times, receive for their Services a Compensation which shall not be diminished during their Continuance in Office.

Section 2

The judicial Power shall extend to all Cases, in Law and Equity, arising under this Constitution, the Laws of the United States, and Treaties made, or which shall be made, under their Authority; to all Cases affecting Ambassadors, other public Ministers and Consuls; to all Cases of admiralty and maritimeJurisdiction; to Controversies to which the United States shall be a Party; to Controversies between two or more States; between a State and Citizens of another State; between Citizens of different States; between Citizens of the same State claiming Lands under Grants of different States, and between a State, or the Citizens thereof, and foreign States, Citizens or Subjects.

In all Cases affecting Ambassadors, other public Ministers and Consuls, and those in which a State shall be Party, the supreme Court shall have originalJurisdiction. In all the other Cases before mentioned, the supreme Court shall have appellate Jurisdiction, both as to Law and Fact, with such Exceptions, and under such Regulations as the Congress shall make.

The Trial of all Crimes, except in Cases of Impeachment, shall be by Jury; and such Trial shall be held in the State where the said Crimes shall have been committed; but when not committed within any State, the Trial shall be at such Place or Places as the Congress may by Law have directed.

Section 3

Treason against the United States, shall consist only in levying War against them, or in adhering to their Enemies, giving them Aid and Comfort. No Person shall be convicted of Treason unless on the Testimony of two Witnesses to the same overt Act, or on Confession in open Court.

The Congress shall have power to declare the Punishment of Treason, but no Attainder of Treason shall work Corruption of Blood, or Forfeiture except during the Life of the Person attainted.

Article 4.

Section 1

Full Faith and Credit shall be given in each State to the public Acts, Records, and judicial Proceedings of every other State. And the Congress may by general Laws prescribe the Manner in which such Acts, Records and Proceedings shall be proved, and the Effect thereof.

Section 2

The Citizens of each State shall be entitled to all Privileges and Immunities of Citizens in the several States.

A Person charged in any State with Treason, Felony, or other Crime, who shall flee from Justice, and be found in another State, shall on demand of the executive Authority of the State from which he fled, be delivered up, to be removed to the State having Jurisdiction of the Crime.

No Person held to Service or Labour in one State, under the Laws thereof, escaping into another, shall, in Consequence of any Law or Regulation therein, be discharged from such Service or Labour, But shall be delivered up on Claim of the Party to whom such Service or Labour may be due.

Section 3

New States may be admitted by the Congress into this Union; but no new States shall be formed or erected within the Jurisdiction of any other State; nor any State be formed by the Junction of two or more States, or parts of States, without the Consent of the Legislatures of the States concerned as well as of the Congress.

The Congress shall have Power to dispose of and make all needful Rules and Regulations respecting the Territory or other Property belonging to the United States; and nothing in this Constitution shall be so construed as to Prejudice any Claims of the United States, or of any particular State.

Section 4

The United States shall guarantee to every State in this Union a Republican Form of Government, and shall protect each of them against Invasion; and onApplication of the Legislature, or of the Executive (when the Legislature cannot be convened) against domestic Violence.

Article 5.

The Congress, whenever two thirds of both Houses shall deem it necessary, shall propose Amendments to this Constitution, or, on the Application of the Legislatures of two thirds of the several States, shall call a Convention for proposing Amendments, which, in either Case, shall be valid to all Intents and Purposes, as part of this Constitution, when ratified by the Legislatures of three fourths of the several States, or by Conventions in three fourths thereof, as the one or the other Mode of Ratification may be proposed by the Congress; Provided that no Amendment which may be made prior to the Year One thousand eight hundred and eight shall in any Manner affect the first and fourth Clauses in the Ninth Section of the first Article; and that no State, without its Consent, shall be deprived of its equal Suffrage in the Senate.

Article 6.

All Debts contracted and Engagements entered into, before the Adoption of this Constitution, shall be as valid against the United States under this Constitution, as under the Confederation.

This Constitution, and the Laws of the United States which shall be made in Pursuance thereof; and all Treaties made, or which shall be made, under theAuthority of the United States, shall be the supreme Law of the Land; and the Judges in every State shall be bound thereby, any Thing in the Constitution orLaws of any State to the Contrary notwithstanding.

The Senators and Representatives before mentioned, and the Members of the several State Legislatures, and all executive and judicial Officers, both of the United States and of the several States, shall be bound by Oath or Affirmation, to support this Constitution; but no religious Test shall ever be required as a Qualification to any Office or public Trust under the United States.

Article 7.

The Ratification of the Conventions of nine States, shall be sufficient for the Establishment of this Constitution between the States so ratifying the Same.

Done in Convention by the Unanimous Consent of the States present the Seventeenth Day of September in the Year of our Lord one thousand seven hundred and Eighty seven and of the Independence of the United States of America the Twelfth. In Witness whereof We have hereunto subscribed our Names.

George Washington - President and deputy from Virginia

New Hampshire - John Langdon, Nicholas Gilman

Massachusetts - Nathaniel Gorham, Rufus King

Connecticut - William Samuel Johnson, Roger Sherman

New York - Alexander Hamilton

New Jersey - William Livingston, David Brearley, William Paterson, Jonathan Dayton

Pennsylvania - Benjamin Franklin, Thomas Mifflin, Robert Morris, George Clymer, Thomas Fitzsimons, Jared Ingersoll, James Wilson, Gouvernour Morris

Delaware - George Read, Gunning Bedford Jr., John Dickinson, Richard Bassett, Jacob Broom

Maryland - James McHenry, Daniel of St Thomas Jenifer, Daniel Carroll

Virginia - John Blair, James Madison Jr.

North Carolina - William Blount, Richard Dobbs Spaight, Hugh Williamson

South Carolina - John Rutledge, Charles Cotesworth Pinckney, Charles Pinckney, Pierce Butler

Georgia - William Few, Abraham Baldwin

Attest: William Jackson, Secretary

Amendment 1

Congress shall make no law respecting an establishment of religion, or prohibiting the free exercise thereof; or abridging the freedom of speech, or of the press; or the right of the people peaceably to assemble, and to petition the Government for a redress of grievances.

Amendment 2

A well regulated Militia, being necessary to the security of a free State, the right of the people to keep and bear Arms, shall not be infringed.

Amendment 3

No Soldier shall, in time of peace be quartered in any house, without the consent of the Owner, nor in time of war, but in a manner to be prescribed by law.

Amendment 4

The right of the people to be secure in their persons, houses, papers, and effects, against unreasonable searches and seizures, shall not be violated, and no Warrants shall issue, but upon probable cause, supported by Oath or affirmation, and particularly describing the place to be searched, and the persons or things to be seized.

Amendment 5

No person shall be held to answer for a capital, or otherwise infamous crime, unless on a presentment or indictment of a Grand Jury, except in cases arising in the land or naval forces, or in the Militia, when in actual service in time of War or public danger; nor shall any person be subject for the same offense to be twice put in jeopardy of life or limb; nor shall be compelled in any criminal case to be a witness against himself, nor be deprived of life, liberty, or property, without due process of law; nor shall private property be taken for public use, without just compensation.

Amendment 6

In all criminal prosecutions, the accused shall enjoy the right to a speedy and public trial, by an impartial jury of the State and district wherein the crime shall have been committed, which district shall have been previously ascertained by law, and to be informed of the nature and cause of the accusation; to be confronted with the witnesses against him; to have compulsory process for obtaining witnesses in his favor, and to have the Assistance of Counsel for his defence.

Amendment 7

In Suits at common law, where the value in controversy shall exceed twenty dollars, the right of trial by jury shall be preserved, and no fact tried by a jury, shall be otherwise re-examined in any Court of the United States, than according to the rules of the common law.

Amendment 8

Excessive bail shall not be required, nor excessive fines imposed, nor cruel and unusual punishments inflicted.

Amendment 9

The enumeration in the Constitution, of certain rights, shall not be construed to deny or disparage others retained by the people.

Amendment 10

The powers not delegated to the United States by the Constitution, nor prohibited by it to the States, are reserved to the States respectively, or to the people.

Amendment 11

The Judicial power of the United States shall not be construed to extend to any suit in law or equity, commenced or prosecuted against one of the United States by Citizens of another State, or by Citizens or Subjects of any Foreign State.

Amendment 12

The Electors shall meet in their respective states, and vote by ballot for President and Vice-President, one of whom, at least, shall not be an inhabitant of the same state with themselves; they shall name in their ballots the person voted for as President, and in distinct ballots the person voted for as Vice-President, and they shall make distinct lists of all persons voted for as President, and of all persons voted for as Vice-President and of the number of votes for each, which lists they shall sign and certify, and transmit sealed to the seat of the government of the United States, directed to the President of the Senate;

The President of the Senate shall, in the presence of the Senate and House of Representatives, open all the certificates and the votes shall then be counted;

The person having the greatest Number of votes for President, shall be the President, if such number be a majority of the whole number of Electors appointed; and if no person have such majority, then from the persons having the highest numbers not exceeding three on the list of those voted for as President, the House of Representatives shall choose immediately, by ballot, the President. But in choosing the President, the votes shall be taken by states, the representation from each state having one vote; a quorum for this purpose shall consist of a member or members from two-thirds of the states, and a majority of all the states shall be necessary to a choice. And if the House of Representatives shall not choose a President whenever the right of choice shall devolve upon them, before the fourth day of March next following, then the Vice-President shall act as President, as in the case of the death or other constitutional disability of the President.

The person having the greatest number of votes as Vice-President, shall be the Vice-President, if such number be a majority of the whole number of Electors appointed, and if no person have a majority, then from the two highest numbers on the list, the Senate shall choose the Vice-President; a quorum for the purpose shall consist of two-thirds of the whole number of Senators, and a majority of the whole number shall be necessary to a choice. But no person constitutionally ineligible to the office of President shall be eligible to that of Vice-President of the United States.

Amendment 13

1. Neither slavery nor involuntary servitude, except as a punishment for crime whereof the party shall have been duly convicted, shall exist within the United States, or any place subject to their jurisdiction.

2. Congress shall have power to enforce this article by appropriate legislation.

Amendment 14

1. All persons born or naturalized in the United States, and subject to the jurisdiction thereof, are citizens of the United States and of the State wherein they reside. No State shall make or enforce any law which shall abridge the privileges or immunities of citizens of the United States; nor shall any State deprive any person of life, liberty, or property, without due process of law; nor deny to any person within its jurisdiction the equal protection of the laws.

2. Representatives shall be apportioned among the several States according to their respective numbers, counting the whole number of persons in each State, excluding Indians not taxed. But when the right to vote at any election for the choice of electors for President and Vice-President of the United States, Representatives in Congress, the Executive and Judicial officers of a State, or the members of the Legislature thereof, is denied to any of the male inhabitants of such State, being twenty-one years of age, and citizens of the United States, or in any way abridged, except for participation in rebellion, or other crime, the basis of representation therein shall be reduced in the proportion which the number of such male citizens shall bear to the whole number of male citizens twenty-one years of age in such State.

3. No person shall be a Senator or Representative in Congress, or elector of President and Vice-President, or hold any office, civil or military, under the United States, or under any State, who, having previously taken an oath, as a member of Congress, or as an officer of the United States, or as a member of any State legislature, or as an executive or judicial officer of any State, to support the Constitution of the United States, shall have engaged in insurrection or rebellion against the same, or given aid or comfort to the enemies thereof. But Congress may by a vote of two-thirds of each House, remove such disability.

4. The validity of the public debt of the United States, authorized by law, including debts incurred for payment of pensions and bounties for services in suppressing insurrection or rebellion, shall not be questioned. But neither the United States nor any State shall assume or pay any debt or obligation incurred in aid of insurrection or rebellion against the United States, or any claim for the loss or emancipation of any slave; but all such debts, obligations and claims shall be held illegal and void.

5. The Congress shall have power to enforce, by appropriate legislation, the provisions of this article.

Amendment 15

1. The right of citizens of the United States to vote shall not be denied or abridged by the United States or by any State on account of race, color, or previous condition of servitude.

2. The Congress shall have power to enforce this article by appropriate legislation.

Amendment 16

The Congress shall have power to lay and collect taxes on incomes, from whatever source derived, without apportionment among the several States, and without regard to any census or enumeration.

Amendment 17

The Senate of the United States shall be composed of two Senators from each State, elected by the people thereof, for six years; and each Senator shall have one vote. The electors in each State shall have the qualifications requisite for electors of the most numerous branch of the State legislatures.

When vacancies happen in the representation of any State in the Senate, the executive authority of such State shall issue writs of election to fill such vacancies: Provided, That the legislature of any State may empower the executive thereof to make temporary appointments until the people fill the vacancies by election as the legislature may direct.

This amendment shall not be so construed as to affect the election or term of any Senator chosen before it becomes valid as part of the Constitution.

Amendment 18

1. After one year from the ratification of this article the manufacture, sale, or transportation of intoxicating liquors within, the importation thereof into, or the exportation thereof from the United States and all territory subject to the jurisdiction thereof for beverage purposes is hereby prohibited.

2. The Congress and the several States shall have concurrent power to enforce this article by appropriate legislation.

3. This article shall be inoperative unless it shall have been ratified as an amendment to the Constitution by the legislatures of the several States, as provided in the Constitution, within seven years from the date of the submission hereof to the States by the Congress.

Amendment 19

The right of citizens of the United States to vote shall not be denied or abridged by the United States or by any State on account of sex.

Congress shall have power to enforce this article by appropriate legislation.

Amendment 20

1. The terms of the President and Vice President shall end at noon on the 20th day of January, and the terms of Senators and Representatives at noon on the 3d day of January, of the years in which such terms would have ended if this article had not been ratified; and the terms of their successors shall then begin.

2. The Congress shall assemble at least once in every year, and such meeting shall begin at noon on the 3d day of January, unless they shall by law appoint a different day.

3. If, at the time fixed for the beginning of the term of the President, the President elect shall have died, the Vice President elect shall become President. If a President shall not have been chosen before the time fixed for the beginning of his term, or if the President elect shall have failed to qualify, then the Vice President elect shall act as President until a President shall have qualified; and the Congress may by law provide for the case wherein neither a President elect nor a Vice President elect shall have qualified, declaring who shall then act as President, or the manner in which one who is to act shall be selected, and such person shall act accordingly until a President or Vice President shall have qualified.

4. The Congress may by law provide for the case of the death of any of the persons from whom the House of Representatives may choose a President whenever the right of choice shall have devolved upon them, and for the case of the death of any of the persons from whom the Senate may choose a Vice President whenever the right of choice shall have devolved upon them.

5. Sections 1 and 2 shall take effect on the 15th day of October following the ratification of this article.

6. This article shall be inoperative unless it shall have been ratified as an amendment to the Constitution by the legislatures of three-fourths of the several States within seven years from the date of its submission.

Amendment 21

1. The eighteenth article of amendment to the Constitution of the United States is hereby repealed.

2. The transportation or importation into any State, Territory, or possession of the United States for delivery or use therein of intoxicating liquors, inviolation of the laws thereof, is hereby prohibited.

3. The article shall be inoperative unless it shall have been ratified as an amendment to the Constitution by conventions in the several States, as provided in the Constitution, within seven years from the date of the submission hereof to the States by the Congress.

Amendment 22

1. No person shall be elected to the office of the President more than twice, and no person who has held the office of President, or acted as President, for more than two years of a term to which some other person was elected President shall be elected to the office of the President more than once. But this Article shall not apply to any person holding the office of President, when this Article was proposed by the Congress, and shall not prevent any person who may be holding the office of President, or acting as President, during the term within which this Article becomes

operative from holding the office of President or acting as President during the remainder of such term.

2. This article shall be inoperative unless it shall have been ratified as an amendment to the Constitution by the legislatures of three-fourths of the several States within seven years from the date of its submission to the States by the Congress.

Amendment 23

1. The District constituting the seat of Government of the United States shall appoint in such manner as the Congress may direct: A number of electors of President and Vice President equal to the whole number of Senators and Representatives in Congress to which the District would be entitled if it were a State, but in no event more than the least populous State; they shall be in addition to those appointed by the States, but they shall be considered, for the purposes of the election of President and Vice President, to be electors appointed by a State; and they shall meet in the District and perform such duties as provided by the twelfth article of amendment.

2. The Congress shall have power to enforce this article by appropriate legislation.

Amendment 24

1. The right of citizens of the United States to vote in any primary or other election for President or Vice President, for electors for President or Vice President, or for Senator or Representative in Congress, shall not be denied or abridged by the United States or any State by reason of failure to pay any poll tax or other tax.

2. The Congress shall have power to enforce this article by appropriate legislation.

Amendment 25

1. In case of the removal of the President from office or of his death or resignation, the Vice President shall become President.

2. Whenever there is a vacancy in the office of the Vice President, the President shall nominate a Vice President who shall take office upon confirmation by a majority vote of both Houses of Congress.

3. Whenever the President transmits to the President pro tempore of the Senate and the Speaker of the House of Representatives his written declaration that he is unable to discharge the powers and duties of his office, and until he transmits to them a written declaration to the contrary, such powers and duties shall be discharged by the Vice President as Acting President.

4. Whenever the Vice President and a majority of either the principal officers of the executive departments or of such other body as Congress may by law provide, transmit to the President pro tempore of the Senate and the Speaker of the House of Representatives their written declaration that the President is unable to discharge the powers and duties of his office, the Vice President shall immediately assume the powers and duties of the office as Acting President.

Thereafter, when the President transmits to the President pro tempore of the Senate and the Speaker of the House of Representatives his written declaration that no inability exists, he shall resume the powers and duties of his office unless the Vice President and a majority of either the principal officers of the executive department or of such other body as Congress may by law provide, transmit within four days to the President pro tempore of the Senate and the Speaker of the House of Representatives their written declaration that the President is unable to discharge the powers and duties of his office. Thereupon Congress shall decide the issue, assembling within forty eight hours for that purpose if not in session. If the Congress, within twenty one days after receipt of the latter written declaration, or, if Congress is not in session, within twenty one days after Congress is required to assemble, determines by two thirds vote of both Houses that the President is unable to discharge the powers and duties of his office, the Vice President shall continue to discharge the same as Acting President; otherwise, the President shall resume the powers and duties of his office.

Amendment 26

1. The right of citizens of the United States, who are eighteen years of age or older, to vote shall not be denied or abridged by the United States or by any State on account of age.

2. The Congress shall have power to enforce this article by appropriate legislation.

Amendment 27

No law, varying the compensation for the services of the Senators and Representatives, shall take effect, until an election of Representatives shall have intervened.

****

OTHER SELECTIONS by this author.

Listed below are additional tittles of books written and published by T.C. Brennan. All are available either as paperbacks on Amazon.com or as ebooks on Kindle or downloads to tablets.

The UN-AMERICAN President: Barack Obama published in 2011 A detailed account of Obama's first term in office

Faith of A Child: An amusing, tearful and mystical Christmas novel published in 2011-2012

The Killer In My Mind: A gritty, throbbing and very unusual psycho-thriller published in 2015

UGLY TRUTHS About Barack Obama, Hillary Clinton and the REAL Democratic Party. An expose' of the crimes and treachery of Barack Obama, Hillary Clinton and the Democratic Party that most Americans don't know anything about.